A Wo___ ___g

Exercises in Writing

Also by Margreet Dietz

Running Shoes Are a Girl's Best Friend

Powered From Within:
Stories About Running & Triathlon

A Work in Progress

Exercises in Writing

Margreet Dietz

www.margreetdietz.com

ISBN: 14505416 9 0

EAN: 978 14505416 9 5

For Timothy J. Moore

"Every decision you make—every decision—is not a decision about what to do. It's a decision about Who You Are. When you see this, when you understand it, everything changes. You begin to see life in a new way. All events, occurrences, and situations turn into opportunities to do what you came here to do."

Neale Donald Walsch

Contents

Introduction

Introduction

In November 2009 I finished and published my first book *Running Shoes Are a Girl's Best Friend*. It felt like it had been a long and challenging haul since I started working on it in January 2008, shortly after my partner Tim and I moved from Australia to Canada.

Tim is Canadian. I am Dutch. We had lived and worked in Sydney, Australia, for seven years. Quitting our jobs—we both worked as sub-editors at *The Australian Financial Review* newspaper in Sydney—we arrived in Vancouver, Canada, in October 2007. I entered Canada as a visitor and needed to apply for a permanent residency visa before I could work—or stay for that matter.

I have been a journalist since 1996, starting my career at the financial newswire Bloomberg Business News, as it was then still called, in Brussels, Belgium, where I had moved from my native the Netherlands in 1995.

Headquartered in New York, NY, Bloomberg has offices around the world. In 1998 the company owned by Michael Bloomberg offered me a transfer to its office in Toronto, Canada. I jumped at that chance, as I did at the opportunity to move to its stunning Sydney office in June 2000. I left Bloomberg News in 2004 because I was ready for a change. The following year I took a Book

Editing and Publishing course at Macleay College in Sydney before *The Australian Financial Review* newspaper hired me as a sub-editor in 2006. I also began writing freelance articles for a running magazine, *Run For Your Life*.

The first two months after our arrival in Canada, just in time for the 2007 winter, were taken up by starting our lives from scratch here. Tim got a job and we moved into a rental apartment in Port Moody, near Vancouver. (The two-bedroom unit was sparse until our belongings arrived from Australia in January 2008.)

We had also gathered, prepared and submitted the documents for my Canadian permanent residency application. Approval, if given, would take at least six months and without it I could not seek employment in Canada. I decided to use that time to do something I had thought about for years: write a book.

My project started off well. Having decided to focus on female runners and the reasons for their commitment to this active lifestyle, I interviewed 53 women and two top running coaches. I have been a runner as long as I have been a professional writer: this is not a mere coincidence. My experiences as a distance runner have empowered me in every aspect of my life and are an ongoing source of inspiration and motivation. This is what I wanted to convey in my book by merging stories of other female runners with my own.

I had a wealth of material and started planning the structure of the book. This is where my struggle began. After trying different ways of structuring it, I just couldn't seem to find one that worked and kept getting stuck. After a flying start my progress on the book slowed down before coming to a grinding halt. The more I struggled the more I doubted. The more I doubted the less I enjoyed working on my project, before beginning to wonder if all this meant I just wasn't cut out to write books altogether.

Running, as always, cleared my mind. I trained for and raced in two marathons in 2008. As everyone who has attempted to run the distance of 42 kilometres and 195 metres, doubts about one's ability to finish it are never far away. The only way to get rid of the disbelief is to keep going, step by step, and the finish line will be yours. Eventually. So that's the approach I used with my first book too: I refused to give up and kept writing and rewriting, word by word.

In April 2009, I set myself a writing challenge that became the first draft of the book you are reading now. *A Work in Progress: Exercises in Writing* started as a 10-day project, i.e. my plan was to write the manuscript in 10 consecutive days, as an exercise to regain confidence that I could write a book. Seven months later I finished that first manuscript about female runners and published it as *Running Shoes Are a Girl's Best Friend*.

I wrote most of *A Work in Progress: Exercises in Writing* during the time my doubts about my ability to become a book author nearly got the better of me. Many times I felt so lost I almost relinquished the will to keep pursuing it. I felt I lacked time, clarity, ability and, most of all, simple faith.

Yet I persisted and hope this book, my third, will help you do the same.

ONE

REMEMBERING

My first serious attempt at writing a book has been harder than I anticipated. Making the transition from journalist, which I have been since 1996, to author has been challenging, even more so than I thought it would be. Many times I have been on the verge of giving up. My struggle has been stressful for Tim who works from home and who has seen my initial enthusiasm about my book project turn to frustration and desperation. He has been as supportive as possible. One of Tim's key recommendations has been to Just Do It, advice I neither wanted to hear nor helped me—until two books I read helped me see merit in that approach.

The first one was Ralph Keyes' *The Courage to Write: How Writers Transcend Fear*. Ralph's message is that the best writers are anxious, worried and struggle to write. Rather than fighting that concern and allowing the different types of fears we wrestle with overwhelm and stop us from writing or seeking publication, he recommends we accept the angst and use it to propel our writing.

Reading that all my anxieties were a normal part of the writing process, instead of a sign that I didn't have what it takes to become an author, was liberating. I wanted to contact Ralph to let him know who much his book had helped me. Thanks to Google I found Ralph's website and used the contact form to send him a note on March 12, 2009, three weeks before I started on the project that resulted in the first draft for this book:

Ralph, Just a short email to thank you for writing The Courage to Write. *I've been struggling for the past year with writing my first book and started reading yours feeling quite desperate about my seeming lack of progress and my level of anxiety about that.*

Having worked as a journalist since 1996 I thought I knew how to write. And with a topic I am so passionate and knowledgeable about, I didn't anticipate it to be anywhere near as hard as I have felt it to be.

I didn't expect that writing a book, especially a first, was going to be easy. But lying awake at night with a brick in my stomach, wondering why I couldn't do something I've wanted to do for years, was not what I had anticipated. And it made me question whether I really was a writer after all. How could I feel so reluctant and unable to write? William Zinsser's book On Writing Well *had already told me that "A writer will do anything to avoid the act of writing."*

While that helped, it is your book that has changed my entire outlook on the past 14 months and— perhaps more importantly— about the months ahead. It's made me realise that my experience is not abnormal— it in fact may prove that I am a writer (as long as I complete my manuscript and send it to a publisher or 10). After enjoying your book so much that I read it in two days, I've felt so relieved. Today my writing actually made me laugh—it was not perfect but I was able to simply write words to describe an awkward situation and enjoy that process without the nasty critic in my head ruining it. I have no doubt there will be more anxiety and probably sheer terror ahead but I will learn to use it — and know that I am not alone. As a marathon runner I am familiar with turning anxiety into excitement and performance. Even if worse comes to worse, you can still reach the finish one step at a time.

I've never given up in any race, though the desire to do so was strong in nearly every single one of them. I've never regretted finishing, and some of my most cherished memories are those of my toughest and slowest races. And I'm using that approach to completing my book as well. Your book has made me feel so much more positive about getting to that point. Thank you very much, Margreet

Ralph responded the next day thanking me for the note and wishing me well. He mentioned he is a long-time runner too and suggested I might want to friend him on Facebook which he had recently joined. Feeling honoured, I did and saw on his Facebook page a photo of a blanket-sized quilt his wife had created from the book jackets of the 15 titles he has written so far. The image of this quilt has been on my mind often since and inspires me.

The second book that helped me appreciate the value of Tim's Just Do It advice in the struggle with my manuscript was Natalie Goldberg's *Writing Down the Bones: Freeing the Writer Within*. In this book she recommends an exercise that sounds scary and compelling: setting up a spontaneous writing booth at a local bazaar, carnival or rummage sale. "All you need is a pile of blank paper, some fast-writing pens, a table, a chair and a sign saying 'Poems on Demand' or 'Poems in the Moment' or 'You name the subject and I'll write on it'," Natalie says in her book.

She describes how she set up her booth three years in a row at a bazaar. The first year she charged 50 cents per request, doubling it to a dollar the following year. She had a line of people waiting throughout the day, she writes. "My rule was that I filled one side of a piece of standard-size paper, did not cross out, nor did I stop to reread it. I also didn't worry about putting what I said in poetic stanzas. I filled a page like I did in my notebook. It was another form of writing practice... It is practice in unselfconsciousness. Write, don't reread it, let it go into the world," Natalie writes.

An absolutely terrifying and exciting idea that helped inspire the process that led to this book.

Exercise: Think about the very first time you considered writing a book. Describe everything you remember about that moment, how old you were, where you lived, what the topic of the book was, whether you started on it, and what happened to your plan. Remember what it was, and perhaps still is, that held you back from writing that book, or any other, and put this to the page now too with as many details as you can. Do not judge your words and sentences now—just write.

TWO

COMMITTING

The 20,000-word first draft for this book was written in eight straight days (my plan was 10 days but we'll get to this later) starting on April 4, 2009. I wrote it in an effort to get past the growing despair I felt about the lack of progress on the manuscript for my first book, which I had been working on for 15 months by then. I had a superb topic, done plenty of research and gathered a lot of great material, yet felt hopelessly stuck in my quest to complete my first book.

I had trouble writing, judging every word and sentence I thought of as inadequate. I felt lost in all the material and seemed to stumble at putting it together in the way I had envisioned. As the struggle with my first book intensified I got better at finding ways to avoid working on it altogether. I checked my email constantly, wasted time on Facebook, prioritised household chores so that I could leave my desk, read about writing instead of doing any, and prepared job applications.

William Zinsser said in *On Writing Well: The Classic Guide to Writing Nonfiction:* "A writer will do anything to avoid the act of writing." That's exactly what I did. While I took solace in knowing that I wasn't alone in my battle, I wanted progress. I wanted results. I desperately wanted something tangible that proved I wasn't just making this "I am a writing a book"-thing up.

I longed for the moment when I could say, "I have written a book", instead of, "I am working on one", as had been my explanation for 15 months to those asking how I spent my days. My updated resume showed I was working on a book about women who run. I felt I was someone who didn't have a job, rather than someone who could legitimately say she was writing a book. Unless and until I finished that book, *any* book, I'd feel I had spent more than a year unemployed, rather than as an author.

I needed a finished manuscript, ready for publication, to prove to myself and to others that I could write a book. I didn't understand why finishing that first book seemed so impossible. I thought I had all I needed: topic, material, knowledge and skills. Why couldn't I do it? Had I been mistaken all those years, believing I would one day write a book?Several times I had already come very close to throwing in the towel, and still was not far from doing so.

Still, every day I found a spark of hope, a reason and renewed determination to keep at it. This book is the result of an exercise to inspire and encourage myself that I was an author after all. The main draft of this book was written in those eight days in April 2009 and, as you will see in the following chapters, I had planned for it to become my first published book. It did not. Instead, it helped me decide to return to my main book project which I finished and published seven months later as *Running Shoes Are a Girl's Best Friend*. In January 2010 I finished my second book, *Powered From Within: Stories About Running & Triathlon*. It is a collection of features I wrote for four magazines in Australia and Canada over a three-year period, now compiled in one motivational paperback for runners and triathletes.

As I started working on my third book and made plans for my fourth, I also revisited the material I wrote for this project. Reading through my so-called First Shitty Draft (a term coined by Anne Lamott in *Bird by Bird: Some Instructions on Writing and Life*), I realised it wasn't that shitty and that it could help to illustrate a point: focusing on the process is what brings results, rather than the other way around.

I decided to divide this draft into 33 chapters with as little revision as possible to the original text and to add one exercise at the end of each chapter. This book is about writing, not about writing perfectly. If you want to improve as a writer, you must write and then write some more.

The purpose of this book is to show how much writing you can get done in eight days, or in any timeframe you choose, if you make it a daily habit. This is no short-cut: good writing is hard work. Drafts need rewriting and plenty of polishing. That's OK. Before we write well we first need to write—anything. It's that simple.

This book's exercises ask you to write, something writers often struggle with, and I want you to start *today*. It doesn't need to be much. It doesn't need to be perfect, or even any good. If you think you cannot write anything today, I want you to pen or type at least one sentence saying so and provide at least one reason for your inability to comply. (Incidentally, my dictionary doesn't have a listing for *writer's block* but it does have one for *writer's cramp* defined as muscular incapacity of the thumb and forefinger affecting those who constantly write.)

As with many things in life, solutions to big problems can be quite simple. If you want to lose weight, you need to stop eating junk and start eating well, every day and beginning right now. If you want to write a book, you need to stop procrastinating and start writing, right now and right here.

Simple doesn't mean easy—it just means that it is not complicated. To forego your beloved junk food and change fattening eating habits to healthy ones can be tough. However, it is not rocket science: don't eat the pie and stay away from the fries and the pop. When you decide a goal is important enough, you can warrant and sustain the effort to pursue and accomplish it. If you want to write a book, you need to write and keep writing until you find what it is that you want to say. It's as uncomplicated and as challenging as that.

Your next exercise, as below, is important. Set yourself up for success by choosing realistic goals. You're allowed, even encouraged, to challenge yourself but make sure your goals are achievable, consistently.

Exercise: This book is about writing every day, nothing more and nothing less. Decide the number of words you will write daily for at least the next 33 days, in keeping with this book's 33 chapters. (Having said that, there is no need to *read* a chapter day—work through this book at your own pace, one that allows you to *write* daily.)

Choose a goal you can sustain day after day. It's more motivating to start with a number that you find easy to achieve, and perhaps increase along the way, than beginning with an ambitious number that sees you give up because it feels too hard. It's better to achieve 2100 words by writing 300 words in seven consecutive days, than to do them in one day and not write at all the rest of the week. It's all about getting into a daily habit, one that you enjoy.

I want you to write without criticising your words. Remember, this is about writing, not writing perfectly. These exercises are about (re)connecting with the joy of writing, not to set you up for frustration and disappointment. If you write only 100 words a day every day you will have 36,500 words after one year. That's a book.

Now decide what time of the day you are planning to do your writing. If you think you are too busy, get up 30 minutes earlier. Write down your goal and commitment to achieving it every single day. Detail how important this is to you and why. Be specific. Keep writing until you have at least reached your daily word goal.

(If you like, multiply your daily word goal by 33 to determine how many words you will end up with at the end of this book. Most books have about 250 words per page. Then forget about these numbers again—we'll first focus on the process that will get us there.)

THREE

READING

Reading books about writing has been very helpful for me—though I must also admit that at times I have used my need to read as an excuse to not write—and I highly recommend you do too. The information you absorb ferments in your mind and may come together in unexpected ways. That's how the book you are reading now came about.

Yesterday Tim told me he's planning to visit his parents again soon, as he has done about every two months since we moved to Canada. They live on the other side of the country, in Toronto, so when Tim visits them he usually goes for 10 days. That means I am home alone and Tim has often encouraged me to use the peace and quiet to write—perhaps even finish that first book I've been fighting with. As we're discussing his next Toronto visit we joke about how I could write a book, any book, in the 10 days that he will be away.

Getting ready for my daily writing session this morning, I rethink last night's conversation and how desperately I'd like to be able to say that I have finished a book because I lose confidence each time I hear myself explain to friends, family and potential employers that I've been working on one for more than a year, without any idea if and when I will finish it.

For my own sake, I need to have written a book before I lose the belief that I can and will.

I also think about the work and patience still required on my first book and the many lessons I feel I've learned through the 15 months I've been working on it; Ralph's book saying we need to use our anxieties as a writer to help us write; Natalie's spontaneous writing booth; and electronic book publishing. An ebook, or a book in an electronic format, can be published and made available for sale worldwide nearly as soon as it is finished.

Perhaps I shouldn't wait until I am home alone next when Tim goes to Toronto: I can start today and write a book in 10 days. If you believe that to be a strange thought for a writer who has been battling another manuscript for more than a year, I have to agree. What does make sense to me is that those 10 days would give me a break from that manuscript, while I work on a new one.

So here's my plan for the next 10 days: I will aim to write about 2000 words a day. That means I will have 20,000 words at the end of DAY TEN. With a typical book holding about 250 words per page that will give me an 80-page book.

Exercise: Think about the books have you been reading lately. (You have been reading right? If you haven't, head to your local library—if you are not already member please sign up today—and borrow one of the books I have mentioned or any other one that appeals to you.) Describe a topic you like to read about and why, or write about your favourite author and what makes their writing so compelling to you. Be specific and elaborate. Don't judge your writing. Anything goes. The goal is to write. We are focusing on quantity for now. Quality will come. Keep writing until you have reached the daily word goal you set yourself in the previous exercise.

FOUR

PROMISING

The biggest problem with the first book I have been working on, and so happily put aside to do this challenge, has been its structure. I know my first book's key message—running is empowering physically, mentally and socially for any woman—but I haven't been able to organise my material into a format I like and can work with.

My initial plan was to organise the comments and experiences of the 53 female runners and two coaches I had interviewed interweaved with my own around various topics, which would be chapters. I got stuck in the endless number of possibilities.

I tried to apply the advice about creating a structure from Jeff Bollow's *Writing FAST: How to Write Anything With Lightning Speed*. While his book showed how to approach structuring a manuscript, I still was unable to solve the dilemma for mine.

With structure as the key stumbling block I encountered preparing my first book project, I have decided not to worry about that whatsoever in this one. I just want to write about my journey to become an author, one that I realise now started a long time ago. I hope it will inspire you to think about your book in progress and why you haven't written, finished and/or published it yet.

Getting into the habit of writing daily, in the sense of working on a book, has taken me several months, arguably years, but now it is what I do. For this 10-day challenge that will lead to the first draft of this book I will sit down each morning with the goal to write 2000 words.

Every day I will start with an idea that supports the theme of this book, which is that writing is a process, and follow where it takes me. I will type as much as I can, without revising. The key is to consider this approach as a valid and exciting challenge that will teach me how to keep writing without allowing my inner critic ruining my day by erasing my words before I have even put them on the page.

The time to be critical of one's writing comes later, once we have written we can start revising: first, we must put our thoughts onto the page.

Exercise: Describe a problem you feel you have wrestled with in your writing and explain why it has held you back from achieving what you set out to do. Now promise that you will not worry about that issue during these exercises. Put that promise in writing and describe how good it makes you feel.

FIVE

MOTIVATING

My decision to write this book is a decision about who I am: an author.

I have found notes dating my first plans to write a book back to at least 1997. I've had plenty of great ideas which I have yet to turn into a finished and published book. [This was true when I wrote the first draft for this book in April 2009. As of March 2010 I have finished and published two books, *Running Shoes Are a Girl's Best Friend* and *Powered From Within: Stories About Running & Triathlon*. This book is my third.]

I have always had a good excuse. For years Writing a Book was something I was going to do One Day. For years Writing a Book was something I probably didn't believe I could do—and I still don't believe it until I do. For years I didn't have the time—which really means I didn't make the time—to write a book.

Since I love reading and pay regular visits to book stores and libraries, I sometimes feel discouraged thinking about the gazillions of books already out there. Is anyone really waiting for me to write another one?

Exercise: Describe the reason(s) you have not yet completed your book. Be specific and keep writing without judgement until you have at least met your daily word goal.

SIX

PRIORITISING

Writing a book is as big a project as it is simple. You need an idea, you need to make the time to write and, then most important and sometimes hardest of all, you actually need to write.

Ideas have never an issue for me. I've thought of various topics for books over the years. They are great ideas that are just as valid today as when I first considered them.

English did not become my main language until I was 26, and arguably it wasn't until I was 30. Born and raised in the Netherlands, my mother tongue is Dutch. Like all kids in the Netherlands I was taught at least one foreign language in high school. My classes included English, German and French. In university I took Spanish classes for a couple of years. Most Dutch will speak at least a few words in either English or German.

My mother tongue has always felt somewhat awkward to me. That seems strange.

My mother was born and raised in what was then Czechoslovakia. She and my grandmother, *oma* in Dutch, immigrated to the Netherlands when she was 13. My mum speaks fluent Dutch without any detectable accent.

While my sister and I heard her sometimes speak Czech with *oma*, we never learnt the language. As an adult I've often wished we had, though not enough to begin studying it.

Since 2006 I've chosen to learn the language of music, playing guitar and piano keyboard. As a kid I had electronic organ lessons for eight years, so I remember the basics such as reading music. The main part of my curriculum on the electronic organ was church and classical music, which hardly inspired me then. I kept practice for my weekly lessons to a minimum.

In the past four years I have played one of my five guitars or piano keyboard for at least five minutes every day, though without a focused plan I haven't made as much progress as I could have if I had had one. That's OK. I know that if I want to accelerate the development of my musical skills I need to spend more time on it. My daily schedule reflects my priorities: the lion's share is taken up by writing, rewriting and editing.

For most of last year I was an active volunteer for a local visual arts group of which I became a member in February 2009 to exhibit my paintings. I coordinated two art exhibitions and was the group's publicity and marketing director. With 10 exhibitions to participate in as an artist in a year, I also had to create new artwork to display. While my visual art has become an important way of expression since I first tried it in 2005, my writing is far more important to me. I will not renew my commitment as director in 2010 and will likely cut down on the art shows I exhibit my paintings in. It's all about choosing priorities.

Exercise: Write about your schedule. Where does writing rank and why? Describe if you believe your writing gets the priority it deserves. If it doesn't, describe how you can make more time for it or how you can make the time you do have more productive. Be specific.

SEVEN

PORTRAYING

Books have always been an important part of my life, including when I could not read yet. One of my mum's favourite stories is that I asked her to read from my favourite book *Goldilocks and the Three Bears* so often that I had memorised it and recited it with her word for word. Once I learnt to read, books were never far from my hands and I soaked up information.

I was about 11 years old when we were preparing for the arrival of a puppy, after the Border collie my parents had had since I was born had died of old age. My parents had decided an Irish wolfhound would be a good fit for our family and had chosen what they believed and turned out to be a reputable breeder.

Before committing to buying a puppy from this breeder, my parents, sister and I went to meet him and his wife at their kennel. As they showed us around, the breeder told my parents about one of their dogs named Icarus. The breeder's wife turned to me and said, "You probably don't know where that name comes from". I told her that Icarus was a Greek man who had made wings out of wax and fur. He was able to fly but flew too close to the sun so the wax melted, his wings fell apart and he crashed back to earth.

At the local library, which I visited regularly, I looked for books from my favourite publisher, a company called Lemniscaat. Checking their website today I learn the company is named after the lemniscate of Bernoulli. I remember going through the books on the library shelves looking for their figure eight-shaped logo. Without fail, every book published by Lemniscaat I read in a matter of days, sometimes hours.

I've always been a fast reader: especially when the book enthrals me I can barely stop reading until I reach the final page. As a kid I read mostly fiction but as an adult I've been drawn to non-fiction. I have learnt about my favourite topics from books and the shelves of our home library reveal who I am or want to be.

The number of Dutch books is not quite enough to fill one shelf. Included are a few hard-cover copies signed by the authors at the monthly events organised by a literary group Gheraert Leeu in Gouda, the Netherlands. Leeu was a printer and publisher born in Gouda in the 15th century. I joined this literary group's board after I started in my first fulltime job, in marketing research at a car leasing company, after obtaining my Bachelor of Commerce in 1993. It was a good job that I quit two years later because I wanted to become a journalist.

The biggest section in my bookcase by far is the one with books on running, triathlon and mountaineering--it covers two full shelves. I am a runner and hope to be for life, was an avid triathlete and am an armchair mountaineer.

Books about visual art fill the next shelf. There are several books about the Belgian surrealist painter Rene Magritte as well as about abstract expressionism and the painters associated with it including Hans Hofmann and Willem de Kooning.

Books about music, guitar and piano specifically, are found on the shelf below. The next one supports a collection of Lonely Planets to various parts of the world, some that I have used and others I have not yet, and fiction books including Tim Winton's *Dirt Music* and Mark Haddon's *The Curious Incident of the Dog in the Night-Time*. Last but not least are my books on writing including the style guides from Bloomberg News and Fairfax, and the Australian Editing Handbook.

(Auto)biographies are found on each shelf.

Tim loves books almost as much as I do. In our move from Australia to Canada, 30 of our 85 boxes contained books—and this was after we had downsized our collection dramatically. To keep the collection in check, Tim and I have returned to our local libraries, where I found some of the books that helped me most with my writing.

Having said that, one of the main reasons I love visiting New York is for browsing its phenomenal book stores. On a two-day stopover to New York in late 2007 I bought eight books, all on writing and visual art including Zinsser's *On Writing Well* and *De Kooning: an American Master* by

Annalyn Swan and Mark Stevens. The latter is a superb 778-page biography which I read in days. Adding the weight of these books to my suitcase that was already bursting at the seams before it travelled from New York to my next stops in Hawaii on the Big Island and Maui before heading to my final destination Vancouver, Canada, wasn't very logical. But I did so anyway.

Exercise: Describe the collection that graces the shelves in your bookcase and how it reflects who you are and want to be.

EIGHT

UNDERSTANDING

When I lived in Brussels from September 1995 until March 1998 one of my favourite things was walking around the Belgian capital to enjoy the variety in beautiful buildings, such as those created by Art Nouveau architect Victor Horta.

Another favourite was visiting the Museum of Modern Art, then the pre-eminent home of Rene Magritte's paintings. In 2009 a Magritte Museum opened in Brussels which I hope to visit the next time I am in Europe.

I miss Brussels—it's a great place to live.

At the time the first piece upon entering the Museum of Modern Art was a doll sitting on a horizontal plane. At seemingly random intervals, part of this plane would fall away with the doll dropping backwards and its metal head hitting a loud bell as a result. Most visitors were keen to begin their exploration of the museum but this piece stopped them in their tracks.

Nearly everyone felt compelled to wait for the doll to drop—exactly because you were not sure when that was going to happen next. It could take a while and when it did, it happened very quickly. Many people including me spent what felt like an eternity waiting, before giving up. As you walked away, still thinking about the doll and wondering if you should have had more patience, you heard the bell clearly announce the answer.

Many would return to the artwork and resume their wait for the next drop of the doll. Something about this piece, even though you knew exactly what was going to happen, made you want to see it, experience it. All you needed was patience to wait for the art to reveal itself.

In our rushed society, few people have mastered the simple discipline of waiting. I remember neither the name of the artwork, nor that of the artist. But I clearly recall standing in front of it, struggling with my impatience even though I was without any deadlines for my museum visit.

It offers interesting parallels with life.

Often we know exactly what we should do to achieve a goal but lack the patience and perseverance needed to pursue it. It may be a lack of focus, resources, energy, confidence or perception of things possible. I am working hard at being more patient, determined and focused.

There is always an element of chance. Some people arrive at the museum a couple of minutes before the doll is set to perform. Without knowing this, these visitors could decide waiting might take too long and keep moving, only to regret it two minutes later and return for the next performance, whenever that may happen.

Exercise: Write about the role patience, or your lack thereof, has played in your goal of becoming an author.

NINE

ASPIRING

My first published stories I wrote in the early 1990s for an alumni magazine—all were non-fiction. I remember feeling very excited about writing them and seeing them published with my byline.

My first writing I did in diaries. Many of those, mostly haphazard, entries have disappeared during my many moves. One diary that survived is of the first year after I moved away from home at the age of 19 to rent a house with two fellow students. The first entry was on August 23, 1989 and the last one, on the final page of the journal, was on April 23, 1990. It's the longest continuous diary I've kept and that's probably the best thing about it: the writing is bad.

One of my roommates and I also began writing poetry then. We'd take a bottle of wine and a few blankets to the local river in the early evenings and sat along the shore with our notepads, pens, blankets, snacks and cigarettes or roll-your-owns to write. The building of which we rented the top two floors was dilapidated. We spruced up a few walls by adding poetry, including our own, to them with waterproof markers.

When I joined the board of the literary group in Gouda in 1994 some of the poems I wrote in university were printed in a home-made bundle along with those by other board members. We read our respective poems at one of the monthly gatherings our group organised, typically for published Dutch authors to discuss their work.

Invited authors usually brought some of their books to sell. I still have the ones I bought. My favourite inscription is from the late J. van de Walle in a hard-cover copy of a 574-page collection of novels and stories because it reminds me that my choice to take the path I am on now started developing then. Van de Walle, who was in his early 80s then, wrote: "For Margreet, the first girl with an interest in Dada - Breton - Magritte."

I wrote poetry throughout the 1990s. Most revolved around understanding my place in the world and the direction I was headed in. Writing my poems helped me clear my mind by organising my thoughts on paper.

Exercise: Describe the first time you acted as a writer, even if you were not conscious of it then. Write about feelings, imagination and/or daily occurrences. Detail what you wrote, dreamt or thought about back then, why, and how it made you feel.

TEN

ACTING

In 1996 I secured a three-month paid internship as a reporter in the Brussels office of Bloomberg Business News. I was determined to make the most of the opportunity to be a professional writer. A year earlier I had quit my marketing job to move to Brussels because I believed this city offered better chances to succeed in my plan to become a journalist. To justify and focus my first cross-border move I had enrolled in a master's degree in International and Comparative Law at the University of Brussels. The one-year fulltime study had been a major challenge and my successfully completing it gave me a boost of confidence that helped me to deal with the next steep learning curve I faced at the start of my career as a Bloomberg News journalist.

I learnt how to write multiple daily news reports on business and finance in English under tight deadlines. I learnt to Show Don't Tell in my stories, which means saying "Deadlines were as short as 15 minutes," instead of, "Deadlines were tight."

There was so much to work on—I needed to learn how to write about financial markets and to do so quickly and accurately in Bloomberg style, I had to improve my English vocabulary, learn how to use the Bloomberg terminal to find and analyse financial market data and interview traders, analysts, investors and company executives.

I loved it. My three colleagues including the bureau chief were experienced journalists and as keen to mentor as I was to learn.

Soon I was hired as a fulltime reporter. Bloomberg News fulfilled my dream of becoming a professional writer within a year after I quit my marketing job to do so. Over the 7 1/2 years I worked as a newswire reporter, I wrote about bonds, stocks, currencies, monetary policy, the economy and company news on three continents.

The stories I wrote for Bloomberg News were picked up by and published in newspapers around the world. My role also included regular TV slots, both live and taped.

Work took up at least 50 hours a week, usually more. I met Tim through work. Also a journalist, he had started working for Bloomberg News five years before I did by opening its Toronto office. By the time Bloomberg News transferred me from its Brussels office to that in Toronto in April 1998, Tim had moved to Vancouver to open another office there. We met a few times at office functions and found out we were both runners. Tim had finished his first two marathons as I was preparing to do my first in Ottawa in May 1999.

In 2000 the bureau chief of Bloomberg News in Australia offered me a job in Sydney and I didn't hesitate. I celebrated my 30th birthday in business class of a Qantas Airways plane flying from Toronto to Sydney.

Two other colleagues from Canada were offered transfers to the Sydney office and arrived there within two months of me. One was Tim. It was nice to have a colleague with similar interests there. By then we each had tried a couple of triathlons, a sport Australians excel in.

I wasted no time in signing us both up for our first half Ironman, which we did in Forster-Tuncurry in October 2000. It was one of the few triathlons I finished faster than Tim. We did our second half Ironman—in which athletes swim 1.9km, cycle 90km and run 21.1km—in Canberra in December that year. We had so much in common that we became good friends. And started dating at the end of 2000. A year later we moved in together, in between doing those same half Ironman events in October and December.

By late 2003 both Tim and I wanted a change from the fast-paced financial and business news world. By now we were spending up to 30 hours a week training for triathlons. We had finished our first two Ironmans, in which professional and amateur athletes swim 3.8km, cycle 180.1km before running a marathon (42.2km). Preparing for long-distance triathlon races had provided a balance to the demands of working as a journalist for Bloomberg News. Yet we were both tired of our frantic lifestyle which didn't leave much time for anything else than work and triathlon training. Our alarms rang as early as

3:30am on weekdays, so we could swim, bike or run before starting our workdays of at least 10 hours at 8am. We often trained after work too.

Holiday time was 20 days, or four weeks a year. Taking unpaid leave was not an option at Bloomberg News. If we wanted more time off we would have to quit our jobs. At Bloomberg News that meant giving up the opportunity to work for the company ever again—the world's top newswire had a policy then of not rehiring former employees.

Resigning from our six-figure jobs without an option to return to the company or having any other work lined up seemed drastic. We considered our options carefully and started preparing for a plan to travel for 12 months (which had turned into 15 months by the time we returned to Sydney at the end of June 2005).

We moved from our $600-a-week two-bedroom two-bathroom apartment in Bondi Beach to a $325-a-week one-bedroom one-bathroom apartment in Randwick in November 2003. Storage boxes hid one wall of our new living room. When Tim and I moved in together two years earlier because we were sick of lugging triathlon training gear for an entire week between our separate apartments located at the opposite ends of Bondi Beach, we had paid a combined $775 in rent per week which is how we thought $600 a week was a good deal.

Cutting our rental costs nearly in half added to our savings, while the drastic reduction in living and storage space forced us to begin culling our belongings, making it easier and cheaper to put the remainder in storage during our year of travel.

Six months later, in March 2004, we both quit and were walked out the door the same day. When I received my final monthly Bloomberg pay cheque, which was five figures, I wrote on the back, "This pay cheque amount, knowing that I gave it up to chase another dream, makes me feel alive."

Exercise: Describe a decision you have taken that did not make financial sense—at the time or even now—but was important for you to take regardless. Write down everything that you gave up or lost, as well as everything you have gained because of it.

ELEVEN

PERCEIVING

Tim and I had become dedicated triathletes since our move to Australia, the land that has produced world champions such as Greg Welch, Michellie Jones, Chris McCormack and Craig Alexander. We had planned our year off around spending several months with our families in the Netherlands and Canada, something that had been hard to do when we lived in Australia with only 20 days of annual leave as Bloomberg News employees.

We also planned to compete in triathlons in Europe, North America and New Zealand during our sabbatical. While our training and preparation for these races took up nearly the same hours per week as a standard fulltime job, I no longer had to combine this with being a Bloomberg News reporter. I revisited my plan to Write a Book One Day—and decided that I really needed a laptop before I could become an author. Tim had brought his on our travels and of course let me use it too. But to write a book I felt I needed my own.

We had left Australia in April 2004 and travelled to The Netherlands where we stayed with my sister, who then lived around the corner from my parents, for three months. Then we travelled to Canada where we spent another three months at the house of Tim's sister, her husband and three kids in Toronto. In November 2004 we flew to the West Coast of Canada where we rented a studio apartment in Victoria on Vancouver Island. Here I bought my first laptop, an Acer that I am still typing on today. Once I had the key tool I started working on an idea for a book. I did not get far.

I did write, mostly on our blog describing our travel experiences including the triathlon training and races for our friends and family overseas. I enjoyed writing about amateur endurance sports. When I wrote a report on a triathlon Tim and I did in the Netherlands, I decided to send it to the editor of xtri.com, a website popular with long-distance triathletes. It was published there in May 2004.

Exercise: Describe something you are passionate about. Be specific, especially about the reasons for your boundless enthusiasm and the ways it has influenced your life.

TWELVE

PERSISTING

I try to put on my arm warmers in the transition area but I can't. I am unstable and cold. I am so cold. I doubt I can keep my balance on a bike right now. I start shaking so badly that I can't do anything. I am trying to cry but I am too cold. A male official notices that I am not doing well. He takes me to a female official and suggests putting me under a hot shower.

I am still wearing my sleeveless wetsuit and my wet top and shorts underneath. As they turn on the shower, the water is cold. Not as cold as it was in the Nieuwkoopse Plassen during the 2 ½km swim of the 2004 Dutch Championships Triathlon for the mid distance. The female official says you need euros to get hot water and leaves to get one.

As the hot water pours over me, my shaking gets worse. One euro won't warm me up and the woman says she'll get more. I am thinking that this will be my first race with a Did Not Finish behind my name. I don't see how I could last one kilometre on the bike in the windy conditions, given how cold I feel now. To save time I am used to wearing the same outfit during the swim, bike and run. It is made of fabric that dries quickly. Right now all I want are warm and dry clothes.

The woman adds another euro to keep the shower water hot. She and the other official are asking whether I want to continue the race.

I tell them that I do but I also don't want to get sick or fall off my bike because I am still so cold and disoriented. They nod. The woman tells me after the fourth euro that at least I am starting to regain normal speech. Hmmm that's good.

I think about my parents who've come to watch their first triathlon today. They've seen me come out of the water and naturally are wondering why I haven't made it onto my bike yet. Great experience, a frozen daughter. My mum has always been worried about me doing these races.

I decide that at least I will have to get out of my wet clothes and have no other choice than to wear my pre-race outfit. As I walk back from the shower to the transition area, which is awfully quiet by now, I wave to my parents who are anxiously waiting. I go back to the change room and get rid of my wetsuit and wet race gear. I strap on every dry item I have with me; a singlet, a bike shirt, a long-sleeved T-shirt and a big grey sweater, thick track pants and dry socks.

It had been a sunny week and the race website said on Thursday the water temperature was 20 degrees Celsius. However, a cold Friday night and pouring rain on Saturday night lowered it to 16.1 degrees on race morning. As we are waiting for the race to start, competitors are trying to catch rays of the morning sun for some warmth and aim to stay sheltered from the wind.

When it is time to hit the water, I am one of the last to do so. I had skipped my usual warm-up swim to stay warm as long as possible. As I feel the water fill up my wetsuit, I am shocked at the cold.

A start with only 300 competitors shouldn't be too bad, compared with the 1600 we have been used to at Ironman races. The clay ground makes for the darkest water I have swum in. Combined with the cold and a few aggressively swimming fellow triathletes, it is an interesting start to our European racing season.

I tore my swimming race cap as I put it on before the start. Without spares, the race organisers recommended I use a cap of my own. Thankfully the one I brought is of thick material. The water feels very chilly against my face, my arms and my feet. I think of warmth and try to get into a rhythm.

The buoyancy of the wetsuit is great. The first lap goes by quickly, though I am aware of my vulnerability to the cold in a sleeveless wetsuit and with a thin layer of body fat. The swim course is a perfect rectangle, lined by an orange rope and marked by row boats with at least one official every 25 metres. As I begin the final 600 metres I keep my eyes on the boat closest to me because I am not sure I will make it to the next one.

I don't feel disoriented, a sign I know is an indicator of the onset of hypothermia, but I have a limited sensation in my extremities. A few breast strokes make me feel better and I move to the next boat. And the next one, and the next one until I reach the end of the swim course where a wide ladder provides an exit from the water. With a little help I make it into T1 (the swim-to-bike transition area) and have never been happier to finish a swim. And never colder.

To my surprise, the Dutch Triathlon Association official, who has been checking on me in the shower, says that I can continue my race if I want. The driver of the sag wagon is waiting for me. T1 is empty except for the numbered grey garbage bags filled with wetsuits and other belongings of the competitors. Officials have started to collect the bags to transport them to the finish area. I dig up my bike shoes and my helmet but decide not to bother finding my sunglasses in between all my wet gear. My dad is outside, holding my bike and chatting to the driver of the sag wagon.

I am happy the organisers allow me to continue. The marshals directing the athletes and traffic on the course will have to stay until I pass them. Oh well, with my personal truck behind me for the next 84 kilometres, I mount my bike and clip into my pedals. Time to go.

I feel special. And embarrassed too. I have never been dead-last in any race. And it looks like I may retain that special slot. Marshals along the bike course are surprised to see me come through, as all other competitors passed many minutes ago. They quickly get into position to direct me along the course. When I smile and thank them, most shout "Kom op he!" (Dutch for, Keep it up.).

The scenery along the course is pretty, as it follows wide bike paths and rural roads with little traffic. The sun is shining and with the amount of clothes I am wearing, I finally feel warm. My outfit definitely makes for a triathlete in disguise. So much so that when I ride into town towards finishing the first of the two laps, two marshals tell me to turn right before honks from the sag wagon behind me indicate that is probably the wrong way. I stop and ask. "Sorry I didn't think you were in the race," they say. I laugh, adding they cost me precious seconds and head in the right direction.

The bike consists of two laps. The six lead athletes pass me before I finish my first and have started the run when I still have another 42km of cycling to go.

I smile. I am warm. I don't need to worry about keeping the 10-metre drafting distance from a competitor. I have my personal truck following me and my mum and dad are there to cheer me on.

The wind is strong. With a headwind my speed drops as low as 21km per hour, according to my speedometer. If it is behind me I reach 40km per hour. I keep hoping every cyclist I pass is part of the race too, but unfortunately none of them is.

This course has many speed bumps, as do many roads in the Netherlands these days. They are everywhere. Between my parents' home and that of my sister, which are about a kilometre apart, are four speed bumps.

The marshals are all happy to see me on my second bike lap. Guess it may have something to do with the fact that they can leave their positions as soon as I and the sag wagon have passed. I finish the 84km bike course in 2 hours 54 minutes.

In the T2, the bike-to-run transition area, I put on my running shoes and decide to take off my sweater and long-sleeved T-shirt. Unfortunately, I have no other choice than to run in my track pants. The volunteers give me the rundown on the top four finishers. The first female hasn't arrived yet. Here's my chance.

The run is 20km, consisting of four 5km laps. Competitors have to keep track themselves though officials at different positions along the course register your race number when you pass to make sure you can count.

As I start running, a guy on a bike starts riding with me. 'Are you last?' Yes, I still am and with that I have another personal escort. At least I start passing some people now, even though all are at least one lap ahead of me. I know that for a fact because my new friend on the bike asks each one to make sure that he cycles with the competitor coming in last.

My outfit feels reasonably comfortable. I hold my gels in my hand and get into a rhythm. I love running. The course is pretty and flat. Heading out of town, I run along fields with cows and green pastures. It's still windy, especially along the 1 ½-km stretch serving a full headwind.

I start chatting with the cyclist. He tells me he has been a triathlete for six years and focuses on the Olympic distance, or the quarter as they call it in the Netherlands. Because of an injury, he has trouble running so he is training for a 200-kilometre mountain bike race in Switzerland this summer. Earlier this season he swam in the Dutch Ironman-distance race in Almere as part of a team. The water was so rough competitors got seasick, he says.

My parents are standing near the finish area and it is great to see them smile and hear their cheers every lap. The run goes by fast and before I know it I have done almost three laps.

We pass a guy and with that I lose my last placing and VIP-treatment. As I enter the finish area to begin my final lap, I see Tim for the first time since the start. He had a solid race. His official time is 4hrs 52mins 54secs and he places 100th out of the 176 male competitors.

I run my final lap in solitude except for the four male triathletes I pass, and the officials and volunteers along on the course. It is good to see the finish line which consists of a 1 ½- metre wood ramp you have to run up. Ouch.

The female official, who took care of me when I was a little popsicle earlier today, rushes over as she sees me at the line and congratulates me on finishing. I thank her for helping me get back in the race. I am impressed by the kindness of the organisers to let me continue and finish the race even though I was so far behind. They encouraged me to keep going and I am glad I did.

My official time is 5hrs 50mins 38secs, last out of the 15 women and 13 minutes behind the woman ahead of me. I finish more than 90 minutes after the female winner, a pro. As for the men, I passed five of them on the run.

Exercise: Writing is very much like running a marathon or doing a triathlon, as failure only becomes absolute when we give up. Describe how you have persisted as a writer. Detail how you will keep at it and—if you can—why. Write about who has supported you in your quest and what that means to you.

THIRTEEN

EXPRESSING

Our crazy lifestyle of working at least 50 hours a week as newswire journalists while also training up to 30 hours a week for Ironman had been normal for three years when Tim and I quit our jobs at Bloomberg News in March 2004. While our voluntary unemployment, or sabbatical as we preferred to call it, started instantly, we were so used to living our lives in a constant rush that we just kept up the same pace. It took months before we were able to slow down from the habit of hurried multitasking.

Having time to reconnect with family, travel and train for triathlons was inspiring. Nearly a year after quitting my job I decided to try painting. It was February 2005. We were in Taupo, New Zealand, where we rented a house for six weeks and were finalising our preparations for Ironman New Zealand, held in March. After our training was done for the day we explored the area, or just did very little at all. At an office supply store I bought inexpensive tubes of acrylics and oils as well as A4-size paper. Lying on the floor in the living room of our temporary house in Taupo, I began exploring and immediately fell in love with the process of playing with colours and shapes, and responding to what developed in front of me.

When we returned to Sydney in June 2005, my plan was to find work as a sub-editor which I believed to be a natural progression for a journalist

56

with my experience. Potential employers didn't agree immediately and it took another year before I got that job. I used my time to take creative courses including in writing, painting and drawing.

It was painting that really grabbed me and soon our one-bedroom apartment overlooking Cooper Park in Woollahra (Sydney) was overflowing with tubes of paint and canvases. My first painting was accepted for a group exhibition in an art gallery in Bondi Beach within a year.

Exercise: Write about another way of self-expression that you use or appeals to you, such as singing, drawing, dancing or playing the piano. Describe the similarities as well as the differences with how and what you express through your writing.

FOURTEEN

PLANNING

The creative writing course I took in 2005 allowed me to see how much my writing had progressed in my 7 1/2 years as a financial reporter at Bloomberg News. It also showed I had a lot more exploring to do about the kind of writing I wanted to do and, most importantly, what I really wanted to say.

To improve my skills and bolster my resume I spent $3500 on a three-month Book Editing and Publishing course at Macleay College in Sydney, for which I received a Distinction. I didn't expect then that I would first apply those skills to my own manuscripts.

While finding a job as a book editor was not on the cards, I finally landed an interview for a sub-editor role at *The Australian Financial Review* newspaper a few months later. When I write, few readers would know that English isn't my mother tongue. When I speak, my accent is hard to miss which makes for an interesting first impression at an interview for a job revising and correcting articles written by native English speakers.

During that interview I was asked, among other things, why I didn't pursue a career in TV given my experience with that at Bloomberg News. I remember telling them I loved working with written words more than anything else. Whether it was the impression I made, my track record at Bloomberg News or the strong need for another sub-editor at Australia's top business newspaper, I started as one the following month.

The production editor said it would be a trial to make sure I could handle the role. After two days of training on the newspaper's content management system I did my first shifts as a casual newspaper sub-editor. It was June 2006. I loved the work and was soon asked to work most days of the week before being offered a full-time contract.

Working as a sub-editor allowed me the mental space to think as a writer without the constraints of writing in my day job. Endurance sports such as triathlon and running were topics that I was passionate and knowledgeable about.

A few months earlier, in March 2006, I spent a weekend in the Blue Mountains to run the annual 45-kilometre Six Foot Track trail race. I picked up my race package the day before the event. As is the case at most established and popular races, a small expo offered various running-related products including a new magazine called *Run For Your Life*.

The guy manning the *Run For Your Life* booth introduced himself as the publisher and explained the idea behind this new publication before handing us a free copy. A new magazine might need writers I thought and after hesitating a split-second I asked him if he did. He wasn't enthusiastic until I explained I was a professional writer. He suggested I email him my resume.

It wasn't the first time I had approached a running magazine. I'd applied for a job at the Melbourne office of *Runner's World Australia and New Zealand* and had, on another occasion, introduced myself to the publisher of that same magazine with the idea to contribute articles as a freelancer. Both had failed to generate a response.

I sent the publisher of *Run For Your Life* an email with my resume. And soon he gave me my first assignment: a profile about an amateur runner who had competed in each of the 36 Sydney's City to Surf races. This annual 14km event between Sydney's Hyde Park and Bondi Beach draws tens of thousands of runners, making it the world's largest road race. I got in touch with the runner and organised to meet him and his wife for an interview during their visit to Sydney, shortly before they left for the airport to return to the Gold Coast where they had moved a few years earlier.

We sat on a bench outside in the pedestrian-only shopping street of Bondi Junction where they answered all my questions. This story, which turned out great, was published in *Run For Your Life*'s October/November issue of 2006.

Since then I've been a regular contributor of features to this magazine, soon followed by assignments from a triathlon magazine in Australia and endurance sports magazines in Canada once my permanent residency was approved. After publishing my first book *Running Shoes Are a Girl's*

Best Friend I decided to compile a collection of my magazine stories in a 150-page paperback titled *Powered From Within: Stories About Running & Triathlon*, which I published in March 2010.

Back to 2006 which is when Tim started talking about moving back to Canada. I knew he wasn't as settled in Australia as I felt and I understood why he wanted to be closer to his relatives, especially his parents in Toronto. I was reluctant to leave Sydney because I loved living there. I would have to give up my job as a sub-editor at *The Australian Financial Review* and say goodbye to close friends.

I knew it was very important to Tim. And I liked Canada. And I like new adventures. So we decided to move to Vancouver, British Columbia, and started preparing for that big relocation in the middle of 2007. We left Australia in August that year and spent two months making our way to what was to be our new home. We visited friends in Dubai for a week, then stayed two weeks in Istanbul with my sister who had moved there in 2006 for her work. I spent three weeks in The Netherlands with my parents and grandmother, followed by a two-day stop in New York, where Tim's brother lives, before staying two weeks in Hawaii where Tim raced in the Ironman World Championships.

We arrived in Vancouver at the end of October 2007. We each carried a big suitcase and laptop, as well as Tim's bike and one of my guitars. The rest of our belongings came via sea and we didn't see those until January 2008. Within two months of our arrival, Tim had found a job and we moved into a $1200-a-month two-bedroom rental apartment in Port Moody, near Vancouver. We had also applied for my Canadian permanent residency visa as a spouse of a Canadian citizen and realised it would probably take at least six months before I'd be allowed to seek employment.

So after thinking on and off about writing a book for more than 10 years, I found myself without any excuses to put it off any further: I had the time to write, I had a space to write, I had a laptop and I had a great idea. It was as exciting as it was scary. This was it. I was really going to try to write a book.

Exercise: Perhaps you may not be about to find yourself with a few months to spare like I did. But can you take a holiday to work on your book? Can you take a sabbatical or unpaid leave? Write about potential opportunities for you to make time to focus on writing and finishing your book. Let your imagination run. Writing it down doesn't mean you have to do it, just that you have to think about it and trust those ideas to the page. How much time could you take? How much time would you need? How would you make the most of that time?

FIFTEEN

REGROUPING

DAY THREE.

An empty page marks DAY THREE of my 10-day writing challenge. After a flying start in the first two days where I surpassed my goal to write 2000 words, I hit a wall on the third day.

I know I tried. I know I typed at least the words DAY THREE. But then I let bad habits get the better of me. I failed to focus and allowed the critic in my head to speak up. I cannot remember the specific details of this day which goes to show that, if nothing else, I could have written about how I felt not being able to write. I could have tried to describe my frustration with the blank page, filling it in the process.

I could have told you whether I slept poorly or whether I felt that I did too much in the previous two days or whether the sun was shining so nicely that I didn't want to be stuck behind my desk inside. I could have simply described the weather, what time I woke up and how I made it to my desk.

Incidentally, my space to write has been all over this house in Squamish where we have lived since September 2008, in different rooms, which is another topic I could have used to fill that blank page. Today, for example, my laptop and I are sitting at the dining table. The first spot I used to write in this house was in one of the three bedrooms upstairs that we had designated as my office. That room looks out over our street and the neighbours that have three dogs, an eight-year-old

German shepherd named Tekaya and two seven-month-old Jack Russells named Bandit and Brandy. Their house backs onto a forest with great trails for mountain biking and walking our dog Luka who we adopted from the SPCA as I did this writing challenge in April 2009 (more about that later). It is because of Luka that we now typically walk the Summer's Eve and Seven Stitches trails in that forest at least twice a week.

Our master bedroom faces south. It's a large space with a bed, headboard and one chair I bought 20 years ago and was reupholstered by my parents. These days it also has Luka's crate but it didn't yet then.

The master bedroom's big window receives the sun as soon as it tops the mountain range around the Stawamus Chief, the world's second-largest granite monolith, of which we see glimpses through the high trees in our backyard. I love the view. In front of this window is where I placed a small desk and wrote most of the 20,000 words that became the manuscript for this book.

You can write about the fact that you feel you have nothing to say and before you know it you have 450 words that are worth reading. This chapter is a case in point. You may rewrite or even scrap them in the revision processes later but you should never need to leave your desk without having written.

Exercise: Pick a seemingly mundane topic, such as today's weather, the view outside the window closest to you, your desk or your office and describe it in detail. Details are essential. They show your unique viewpoint. Everything is worth writing about. Pick any of the above topics and describe anything and everything about of it. If that leads you to another topic or story, follow it and keep writing.

SIXTEEN

INSPIRING

It is the day after I lost a battle with the blank page. Remember that my plan is to write this book in 10 days by producing 2000 words each day. On DAY ONE I was inspired and wrote about 3500 words. On DAY TWO I struggled and wrote about 1500 words. On DAY THREE I didn't write at all. That means that I am starting DAY FOUR about 1000 words short of my average daily target. I'd better be inspired today.

I used to think of inspiration as something that would just happen, a feeling that would suddenly arrive and prompt me to do — write — great things. Often I heard a story or got an idea that made me excited and wanting to share it. As soon as I sat down to convey my thoughts and the feeling that came with it on the page it all went wrong: the words I wrote didn't come anywhere near what I had wanted to say. In fact the exact same topic that got me all enthused sounded banal and boring when I tried to capture it in writing. My inspiration left as quickly as it had arrived.

As a writer you do need that initial bout of enthusiasm, excitement and mental stimulation that comes with the feeling of possibility and the desire to rise to the challenge. And you need to hold on to a part of that motivation to keep you going. It's like committing to running a marathon. You often do so as you're thinking about the glory and accomplishment you expect to feel when you will finish that 42.195-kilometre race. You will be cheered for your efforts, your courage to attempt and your success when you accomplish your goal.

You imagine that personal best you are going to run. You may even beat friends and strangers to that marathon finish. Daydreaming about all the possibilities feels great while you're sitting down, or even lying, on the couch. From that position the thought of running a marathon is just as soft and comfortable as your sofa.

Then it is time for you to start preparing. You need a coach and/or a training program. If are a regular runner, you have to train at least four months for a marathon. As a novice runner, you should take a year or longer to get your body in shape for the event inspired by the legend of the messenger who in 490 BC ran about 40km from Marathon to Athens to bring news of Greek victory over the Persians.

You must make the time in your daily schedule to complete the training and commit to doing so consistently. Your training will not always be easy. It will not always be fun. You may have to run outside when it rains on days that you do not feel like doing so. You may have to get up early to fit in that training session before going to work. You'll probably have to run on a day you'd rather be doing something else—like lying on that couch.

Running a marathon is tough and absolutely exhilarating. There are no guarantees except that it will be a challenge, no matter how many you have already done. Yet (almost) anyone can do it if they choose to apply themselves to reaching that goal by training consistently.

Dreaming about it will not increase your fitness any more than thinking about the published book with your name on the cover will fill the blank pages in front of you and improve your skills as a writer. You need that initial excitement, that big goal and you should relish the rush you feel about the thought of achieving it. Then you need to start working. The only way you will complete a book is by writing—word after word, day after day.

Dreams are fundamental to our lives. We must have dreams, wishes and desires. Those are where our inspiration comes from. Inspiration is sustained and strengthened by pursuing your goals through action. If your wish is to write and publish a book, you have to commit to writing. You have to find the time and you must find the mental and physical energy. You need to enlist your spouse, your children, your parents and your friends to support you—mentally or physically.

Like training for a marathon, writing a book won't be easy and it won't always be fun. That's OK because a challenge means to test one's abilities or resources in a demanding but stimulating undertaking. The reason you choose this goal justifies the commitment and sacrifices you have to make to accomplish it. Your results are determined by your efforts.

Exercise: Describe what inspires you. As always, be specific. Write about the reason(s) you bought this book and are doing these exercises. Write about your drive to write. Any and all reasons are valid. We sometimes do not realise how we are inspired to do the things we choose to do. Keep writing, and keep exploring. Discovering more about our own drive to pursue our goals will help us strengthen our commitment to achieving them.

SEVENTEEN

FOCUSING

As I mentioned in the previous chapters, DAY THREE of my 10-day challenge left me with nothing to show for while I had so much I could have written about, particularly how I felt facing the page that is dreaded when it remains blank. We always have a reason for not writing, even calling it writer's block.

I believe that for most of us an inability to produce any writing is fundamentally caused by fear. If we set our expectations too high too soon we can never meet them and lose heart trying. The answer lies in adjusting our goals. Lowering our expectations doesn't mean we lower our standards: we just need to bring our short-term goals closer to our current level of ability in order to move forward towards further improvement.

If we truly can think of nothing to write about, we can encourage expressing ourselves on the page by describing in detail our perceived sense of failure. One word and one sentence at a time— which I wish I had done on DAY THREE. One of my excuses for leaving yesterday's page blank was my training for a marathon. This race is four weeks away. The key marathon training session is the weekly long run which is what I did yesterday morning.

The more years you have been running consistently, the more long runs your body can handle in the five months it takes to prepare for a marathon. Generally, any runner shouldn't run longer than three hours in one session. In my preparation for the Vancouver Marathon, the one I will race in four weeks, I did five of those three-hour runs in the last two months.

I have done more than 50 three-hour training runs since I started running in 1996 and doing triathlons in 1999. These long sessions rarely, if ever, feel easy. Yesterday exhaustion set in during the final 30 minutes of that three-hour run as it usually does. My legs were sore, even more so once I was done running. After a shower and sitting down for two hours I felt better. I could, and should, have worked on filling a page then.

Instead, Tim and I decided to call a good friend in London. We met Stephen seven years ago when the three of us were training with the same triathlon coach in Sydney. We did much of our training for Ironmans together—when you go for a 180-kilometre bike ride together, you have a lot of time to chat. If we travelled to a triathlon race we often shared accommodation with Stephen and he came to Hawaii to watch Tim compete in the Ironman World Championships in October 2007.

He and his partner were among the first friends to visit us in Canada after we moved here from Australia, shortly before they moved from Sydney to London. Stephen took a break from triathlon training for a couple of years until he recently felt inspired to resume it.

Tim and Stephen are following a similar, yet personalised, training program designed by Kristian, a good friend and a coach who is based in Australia. Triathletes can discuss the topic of triathlon endlessly, especially when it comes to training and racing. Our call with Stephen was a fun one that ended after an hour. I could have committed to writing my daily 2000 words then.

Instead, I chose to spend my time making a decision about adopting a puppy we had seen on the BC SPCA website. Tim and I drove to the SPCA office in Squamish, planning to ask for advice. The small building was busy. The puppy we were interested in was there too.

The BC SPCA website has a searchable online database with pets available for adoption across the province. I had been keeping an eye on the website for a few weeks. When I checked the site again two days ago, on a Friday evening, the image of a black and white puppy I hadn't seen before appeared in my search.

I click on the link to see more information about this puppy, named Chewbacca, and fall in love instantly. Then I notice his listing is from our local SPCA branch. My heart jumps—this may be our dog. He is perfect in the way love at first sight makes someone flawless. And he's right here in Squamish.

Tim is out for a run. When I hear him at the front door, I ask him to come upstairs immediately because I have something to show him. Tim quickly takes off his running shoes and follows me to the computer in my office to look at the picture of the puppy (who later that night is temporarily baptised Fred). "Look at him," I say as I jump up and down. Tim agrees. "He's very cute."

We spend the rest of the night talking about how adopting a dog, a puppy, would change our life and if we are ready for the responsibility. The fact that we have recently bought a house doesn't necessarily mean we have stopped being nomads at heart so we need to make sure that we are ready for the commitment a dog requires.

Fred's picture is striking: he looks right at the camera with a slightly tilted head. He reminds me of my sister's Jack Russell. He looks alert and energetic. And that's exactly what he is like when we meet him at the SPCA office two days later, on DAY THREE of my writing challenge.

Black-and-white puppy Fred is bigger than he appeared in the photo. Based on his teeth, the SPCA says, he's probably 3 ½ months old. He is possibly a cross between a Labrador retriever and a pointer, according to the SPCA. (It later turns out the vet classified him as a Border collie cross, a breed requiring even more mental and physical exercise than the other two mentioned above.)

Fred is the centre of attention in the SPCA office. We learn that he has been in a foster family for a week and his foster mom, who arrives shortly after we do to take him home because the SPCA office is closing for the day, says he's a great dog. She says she would have kept him if she didn't have a one-year-old baby.

Meeting Fred just confirms my impression of him: he seems sweet, good-natured, very energetic and a perfect match. If we adopt Fred he will be part of our family for the rest of his life which could be up to 15 years. He will depend on Tim and I. It's a serious commitment.

Exercise: Describe the distractions you allow to keep you from writing. Write about the most common ones and the most unusual ones.

EIGHTEEN

SAFEGUARDING

In the middle of my writing session today my mum calls from the Netherlands, after my sister Angelique had phoned earlier this morning from her home in Istanbul, Turkey.

It's 3:15pm when I resume writing after these two phone calls totalling about 2 ½ hours. It can be challenging to ensure our work hours as authors in a home office are respected. It's up to me to manage my time and people's awareness of my commitment to writing, as if I worked in any other fulltime job: no one would expect me to be able to make a personal phone call for an hour there.

We have to safeguard our writing time. For me it works best when I get up at 6am, make coffee and head for my desk. I usually check my email and a few websites first, even though I know from experience that the risk of distraction is high. If I start responding to emails, my prime writing time of the day flies by without me doing much work on manuscripts at all. And that is exactly what has happened to me in the past two days.

It's early April. I decide to work outside today as the weather is beautiful. I am sitting on the deck in our backyard wearing a hat to protect my face from the sun and a blanket to stay warm when the trees catch the rays instead of me.

I feel better as the days increase in length and become more conducive to spending time outdoors. Few smells beat the one that says spring has arrived with the promise of a warm summer and a colourful fall. Winter has its colours too, especially when a fresh layer of snow covers any messy yards with white perfection. I crave sunlight, especially after living in Australia for seven years.

In Sydney my painting studio was outside, on the balcony of our one-bedroom apartment facing north (which in the southern hemisphere means the sunny side) and overlooking a park favoured by Kookaburras. I love feeling the sun warm my face and body, I love how the sun makes the world feel like a happier place.

Living in Australia, I had a permanent tan as my skin responds quickly to the sun and I swam, cycled or ran outside nearly every day. Sunshine and laughter have left their marks in my face which I've only recently begun worrying about. I could have been more vigilant about protecting my skin by wearing sunscreen and hats. After cycling and running for up to nine hours I usually thought about lying down on the soft sand of a beach after a dip in the cool ocean, eating omelettes and drinking coffee, rather than about blocking ultraviolet rays.

Today, I am listening to my iPod as I sit on two plastic Muskoka deck chairs facing each other. My feet are hidden in pale-brown Ugg boots which is where they have been nearly every day since I bought them in Bondi Junction, Australia, in August 2007. When my feet are warm so am I. My mum always told my sister and I to put something on our feet to avoid a bladder infection. I only wear my Ugg boots at home which is where I've spent most of my time since moving to Canada. The soles are nearly worn away at the toe area.

The rest of my outfit is green, varying in hue from an army tone to a bright apple one, like the fleece Navy sweater I've been wearing most days of the week since Tim gave it to me for Christmas in December 2007. It has several small spots of acrylic paint in the linen shade of the freshly-painted walls of our house, and is warm and comfortable. Underneath it is a soft army-green long-sleeve T-shirt that has a small light-blue moose logo. I bought it in Kuala Lumpur in February 2006 where we stayed a few days after Tim competed in his first Ironman Malaysia, dubbed The Toughest Show on Earth, on the island of Langkawi. He did that race again in 2007.

As my left knee is still heeling from a nasty abrasion suffered in a fall during a run 10 days ago I am wearing shorts. Those I bought in Istanbul, Turkey, in September 2007 and I love them. The Polysporin cream I put on my knee wounds may have ruined these shorts with stripes in various shades of green and dark blue.

My hat is light beige and is also from my visit to Istanbul in September 2007. It was 5YTL (as the Turkish currency was called then), about $3. I wish I'd bought the black version too—I love this hat and have had many compliments wearing it.

My sunglasses, by Prada, are from a store in Sydney in 2007 where they were $200 after a 50-percent discount. I bought them because I liked the way they fit and suit my face. I was also fed up with the $20 pairs that never last more than a month or two. These Pradas I've accidentally dropped many times, yet they are still in one piece and nearly free of scratches.

As always, I wear a pair of small diamond studs set in white gold which I purchased on eBay to replace another pair of superior size and quality after I had lost one of them during a half-hour run in Woollahra. Those larger and more expensive studs I bought in 2004 from a long-time diamond trader in Manhattan and recommended by a friend. The trader had told me he gave me a great deal because of the referral. Not until I lost one and tried to replace it did I realise how true that was. That first pair of diamond earrings had screw tops for safety and I wore them all the time including during training and racing.

That day I came home after running one of my regular routes in the neighbourhood—a lap of about 6km. When I habitually reached for my ears to check if my studs were still securely tightened one ear was naked. I ran to the bathroom mirror as if my fingers failed me but the earring was gone. I searched our apartment, then the hallway and staircase of our building and made a brief attempt to start searching along my running route. It could have disappeared anywhere along those 6km.

I didn't find it. I had owned the earrings for only about a year before I lost one. I knew I wouldn't be able to justify spending the money required to replace it with the same size and quality. The pair of diamond studs I later secured on eBay cost $300 including shipment for a pair of 0.4 carat, SI (slightly included) quality, H colour. While they do not compare with the ones I had bought in New York, I love them and have worn them every day since.

Exercise: Use words to paint a picture of where you are and what you look like right now. Describe your surroundings, what you are wearing, the weather, anything and everything that will give someone else a mental image of your 'here and now'. No one else is in this moment and you will likely forget it too—safeguard it with a detailed description on your page or screen in front of you.

NINETEEN

COINCIDING

I usually write early in the morning because that's when my mind feels fresh and focused. Today I am writing at 5pm in an effort to meet my daily word goal. In my previous two jobs as a journalist and sub-editor I worked in the afternoon and evening, so I shouldn't limit my writing time to mornings only. The most important habit of a writer is to write, daily. I've learnt to do so in the three months leading up to the writing challenge that became this book. The previous year most of my writing time was then spent avoiding doing any of it.

Now I write and work on my writing skills every single day: I'm convinced daily practice is the key to improvement and writing well.

Through the trees I can see the outlines of the Stawamus Chief, the key feature of Squamish. The Chief's 700-metre face has some of Canada's best rock climbing routes. There is also steep hiking trail to one of the three peaks which takes less than two hours. I've hiked it twice, including once with my sister Angelique, and have seen a few people running up and down that trail too.

Regardless of how you reach the top, the reward is a stunning 360-degree view of mountain peaks, the Howe Sound and Squamish.

We all choose different paths in life too. My route to Canada, to Squamish, to this particular house I now own with Tim, has been as long and roundabout as it has been perfectly straightforward and logical. I won't know if I will stay here, until I decide to leave. I've more often departed from, than arrived at—it's easier to go sometimes. I don't mean to suggest that goodbyes are easy: effortless farewells tend to be escapes. And I've done a few of those, consciously and sometimes unconsciously.

Breaking free has helped me become the writer I am today. I am a writer. I know it. I feel it. And I behave like one by writing, consistently. It has taken me a long time to arrive at this point. Everything and everyone I have moved away from was meant for me to get here, to be a writer in Squamish.

(When I did my final of several revisions of this book in April 2010 I read part of *Het Geheim van de Schrijver* (*The Secret of the Writer*) by Dutch author Renate Dorrestein. In this book about writing she says (in Dutch, the translation is mine): "He [the writer] has a message that is meant for everyone. That message comes directly from the personal history of the writer. Or even stronger, as soon as he sits down to write, it seems to him that his history was meant solely to bring him to this point, to this moment when he starts his book.")

Exercise: Think about your journey to become a writer. Describe decisions you've taken to get to where you are right now. Detail coincidences that occurred. Describe how the universe has conspired to bring you where are you now, writing as a writer.

TWENTY

TRAVELLING

You always seem a little scared, someone said to me when I was 23 years old. The comment annoyed me enough to remember it today, 15 years later.

Quitting my first job without the guarantee of another one was unnerving. Moving alone to another country, and later another continent, was unnerving. Interviewing Richard Branson was intimidating. Starting a marathon and an Ironman was frightening. Committing to writing my first book was frightening. I was scared doing all those things, so I guess he was right.

Fear is nearly always part of pursuing challenging goals, especially for authors. As I get closer to completing this book I am scared that its publication will be met with ridicule. "Who does she think she is, publishing a book with advice on writing? Her own writing sucks. Her advice is no good." Yet I keep going because I believe that someone will find value in this book, in my writing. I focus on the task at hand, page by page.

Word count is my favourite function sometimes, like today—it tells me that I've produced 3138 words already. And I am not done yet. Writing reminds me, again, of my experience with running. As a novice runner it is hard to believe that you will ever be able to jog for an hour, and do so comfortably, let alone do something as scary and crazy as completing a half marathon (21.1km). Or a marathon (always 42.195km).

At first running a kilometre feels difficult. As you stick to your beginners' training program, walking with a gradually increased amount of running, your fitness improves. Slowly but surely. And six weeks later you are able to run 4km—or about 25 minutes—without stopping. With your newfound ability to run, you slowly expand the time and distance of your sessions. You draw confidence from each step, each extra kilometre covered. Once you are able to run 5km, you know you are working towards the fitness to do 10km.

The distance you believe you can run increases gradually. While covering a certain amount of kilometres becomes a target that guides your training, it is never the reason a runner runs. While a focus on the number of words I write per day is not an end in itself, it helps direct my writing. The more we practice the better we get. More importantly, writing consistently strengthens your belief that you are a writer and have the right to call yourself one. The more you believe, the less you fear.

Exercise: There are many ways to undertake a journey. How we choose to travel influences the way we feel when we reach our destination—if we do. Few things are certain. One is: without starting your journey you will not go anywhere. Describe where you feel you are in your travels as a writer.

TWENTY-ONE

EVALUATING

I am starting DAY FIVE on a writer's high. My 2000-word-a-day plan is still on target, thanks to my great output on the first and fourth day.

Writing is not about quantity of course. But we need to produce words on the page first before we can begin improving them with quality as a result. I've been working hard on silencing my internal critic, the voice in my head that tells me every word and sentence I create is not good enough. I know I will have plenty of time to rewrite and revise once my first draft is done. Until then writing is my goal and yours too. Expectations that our writing arrives in perfect shape prevent us from putting anything on the page or screen. We need to trust that it is good, at least good enough for now.

Writing is like running. If you can run two kilometres, you can run a marathon. If you can write a sentence, you can produce a book. It doesn't mean you can run a marathon or write that book tomorrow. Training for a marathon, and writing a book, takes time and effort. You may be able to run a marathon after six months of committed training, though it will be easier and more enjoyable after two years of consistent preparation. By running regularly your body learns to cope and your mind will too. Writing is very similar.

Theoretically anyone who can compose a letter or an email can write a book. The latter takes a lot more work, commitment, practice and focus. Most of all, it takes passion. Passion is what will sustain you through the challenges that will always be there in some form or another, whether it is your first book, second or third. You must set yourself up for success by setting your goals within reach. As you improve, you gradually move your objective towards a new level of difficulty.

I'm about to run my 10th marathon. They don't get easier because, aside from the fact that it's simply a long way to run, I make my goals for them more challenging as I improve through consistent training year in, year out.

The first time I started a marathon, in 1999, my main aim was to finish the race. The time it would take me to do so was of less importance, arguably did not even matter. Until I did actually run 42.195km, I wouldn't know if I could. I had been running for three years by then and knew I could run 10km, 20km and even 30km because I had done so in races and training. And of course the final 12km of my first marathon were the hardest and felt so challenging that I doubted my ability to complete it.

However, the prospect of not finishing—which would mean that I could not run a marathon until I tried again and succeeded—was more painful than any part of my legs and feet, so I kept going. Whether I was running, walking or limping, as long as I was moving forward I would get closer to that finish line. As long as I did not give up I would reach my goal. And when I eventually crossed the finish I knew I had the ability to run a marathon. It had been extremely hard, even felt absurd at times, but I had done it once and could do it again. Confidence makes a big difference.

Two years later I ran another one. With more training, racing and even my first triathlons under my belt, I was fitter and better prepared this time. Or so I thought. It took me almost half an hour longer to finish that second marathon.

In 2003 I ran my third. Like in the other two, I was excited and felt fine during the first 30km of running. Then my legs began hurting more and more until I stopped to stretch (and cry) at about 35km, which I had covered nearly an hour faster than in my previous two marathons.

In the first half of the race I had felt great and kept a steady pace. I had run ahead of Tim who was also racing. As I stood there along the course at 35km, crying while trying to stretch my sore quads, Tim passed me. If I was hoping for sympathy I didn't get any.

"What the hell are you doing? Get moving."

And he kept running.

I realised he was right—I'd been doing too well so far to give up. I gingerly resumed running and soon caught Tim again. In the final 2km Tim and I ran stiffly side by side. He had no qualms about speeding up and trying to drop me. Which of course I couldn't allow him to do given that I'd spent much of the race ahead of him. We ended up crossing the finish line with a fraction of a second between us. My 3:24 time was 54 minutes faster than my first marathon. This race hadn't felt any easier than the previous two, nor any harder. The main difference was practice and experience.

Since then I have run six more marathons [and another three since I wrote the first draft for this book], improving my time and overall placing. As I've gotten faster, I've adjusted my goals. In some ways running a marathon is now harder, in other ways it is easier. Most importantly, I love doing them as each one provides new challenges and new lessons. Eleven months ago I ran a marathon, on the same course I am about do in four weeks, and had very high expectations, planning to finish the race in 3:05 or faster. To do so, I would have to cover the distance nearly four minutes quicker than I ever had before—at my marathon pace that is a difference of about 850 metres.

Before I was halfway the mental weight of my expectations had completely crushed my spirit. My body was performing well, just not quite well enough to meet my goal. Tears were running down my face after 25km. I still had more than 17km to go and was distressed. I couldn't believe I'd thought about placing among the top female finishers—now I doubted my ability to finish. I felt so deflated, disappointed and upset.

All I could do was try to keep going. Failure isn't absolute until we give up. I finished in 3:12, my second-fastest marathon time [my sixth-fastest time as of April 2010] and good enough for 17th female. Yet I felt more disappointed with that marathon than any other one I had run. It took me a few weeks to realise my discontent served no purpose. Sometimes things are what they are. All you can do is learn from the experience and use the lessons to do better next time.

I ran another marathon six months later. My goals were different. Instead of thinking about the outcome, I focused on the process: making each step the best it could be at that particular moment. I needed to support myself mentally instead of doubting myself the whole way. With that approach I set a personal best of 3:07:10. In four weeks I am returning to the course where I felt such great disappointment a year ago. My main goal is to stay positive.

Exercise: Describe the goals you have had for your writing in the past and how they have worked for you. This book is an exercise in setting and working on daily targets, word by word. Re-evaluate your goals and detail how you are achieving them. Your goals must be challenging but not so challenging that they leave you feeling as if you are coming up short every time. If the mental weight of your expectations is crushing your writing spirit, adjust your goals to bring them within reach. If you make any changes, describe them and how they make you feel. You may notice that I assume you have set your short-term goals too high, rather than too low, because that is typically what most writers do. However, if you feel that your writing goals are not challenging you enough please adjust them too and describe how and why.

TWENTY-TWO

IMAGINING

Libraries are amazing. A few weeks ago I became a member of my local one. A driver's license for ID and proof that I was living in the area serviced by the Squamish Public Library was all that I needed. After filling out a form I held a card giving me access to thousands of books—not to mention magazines and DVDs.

Free of charge, I can acquire and bolster my knowledge about any topic I choose. During the first three months of my Squamish Public Library membership, I am allowed to borrow five items at a time before limits on the number of books taken out are lifted. Can you imagine having this type of facility for anything else? Anything you'd like to use at your disposal for up to six weeks without any cost?

Exercise: Describe your favourite aisle in the library. Detail its location within the library and which books you find there. Write about the reason(s) are you drawn to this section. Describe where your pending book will be located, whether it is the same aisle or a different one, and how it will feel to see it there.

TWENTY-THREE

FUELLING

Two months ago I attended a meeting of VISUALS, a group of visual artists based in the Squamish Valley. One of my recently completed paintings had been accepted for an art show I had read about in the local newspaper, *The Chief*, a weekly. The exhibition's curator was a member of VISUALS as were many of the artists in that group show held at the Foyer Gallery in Squamish.

During my first VISUALS meeting I decided to join the group and volunteered to help out with coordinating one of its exhibitions. I also offered to help write and edit any VISUALS materials, which prompted the president to suggest in an email the next day that I take on publicity and marketing. Soon I was a director of VISUALS, wearing two hats: PR & marketing and coordinator of two of the group's four group exhibitions held in 2009.

To help promote a demonstration workshop organised by one of our members, a potter, I offered to write a story about her for the local newspapers. She agreed and we set up a time for an interview. As usual I did my run training in the morning before our meeting was scheduled at her home. It was a speed session, during which I run fast in several repeats aimed for time or distance.

I wasn't focused on running, however. My mind was already at that interview taking place after my training. Failing to pay attention to what I was doing, I tripped on an uneven part of the road while running at full speed. I hit the dirt hard.

Upset, sore and bloody I stumbled back to the car and drove home for a bath that would help clean out the dirt from the wounds on my knees and palms of my hands. I considered cancelling the interview but decided against it. My knees were raw and open so I wore a pair of shorts on a chilly day in March. Driving to her house, I wondered why I had taken on a busy volunteer role on top of writing books, training for marathons, painting, playing guitar and renovating the house we bought six months ago.

Even so, I was looking forward to this meeting. I had admired the images of her beautiful pottery on her website which also mentions the bed and breakfast she and her husband operate in their house, her husband's expedition to Mount Everest and the books he's written.

As she welcomed me in their home and provided an insight into her life, I felt this was one of those moments when the universe conspires to show support for your recent choices. The potter's way of looking at her art, her clear passion for it, and her generous and eloquent way of describing it to a clay layperson was inspiring. Her vision as a potter resonated with me as a runner, a writer and a painter.

The first thing she told me was that her art was functional. Some people might argue that it means her art is not art but the less prestigious cousin craft. I believe it showed her confidence.

She had realised during her Bachelor of Arts study as a teenager that her work would be unique simply because it was conceived by her mind and created by her hands, she said. To her exploration is crucial. All her pieces, which display a wide variety of styles, relate simply because she is the one who created them.

After a two-hour visit that flew by I left thinking that our meeting, focused on interviewing her, had also allowed me to understand more about myself and my passions in art, sport and life.

Exercise: Describe what fuels your desire to write. Start simple, "I write because I can." List any and all reasons you have to write. Keep writing and explore all that drives you as an author.

TWENTY-FOUR

LEARNING

My experience as a financial newswire journalist has shaped me as a writer. Bloomberg News has a reputation for working its journalists hard. And it does—that's why the news service division of Bloomberg LP has managed to catch up to, and has in many ways surpassed, organisations like Reuters and Dow Jones. New York mayor Michael Bloomberg founded Bloomberg LP in 1981, though the company didn't receive this name until 1986.

In 1990 Bloomberg started its news division, still known as Bloomberg Business News when I joined the company in 1996, and appointed Matthew Winkler as its editor-in-chief. The New York-based company now employs at least 10,000 people in more than 135 offices around the world, according to its website.

Clients lease the Bloomberg terminal which is a computer system that provides access to live financial market data including stocks, bonds, commodities and currencies, a seemingly infinite array of analytics, one of the most efficient email systems, and Bloomberg News stories.

Writing for Bloomberg News is demanding. Newswire deadlines are short, numerous and not always anticipated. Any story can break any time and you'd better be the first to report it. Ideally you are the one to set the schedule by breaking the story, with competing news organisations to follow. Time is of the essence. If you're not the first with the news, you're beaten. As a Bloomberg News reporter, you learn to write a four-paragraph story in 15 minutes. On a typical day you write multiple stories, often expanding and updating them with more information as you gather it.

My contract in each of the offices that I worked in between September 1996 and March 2004 specified a workweek of 50 hours, or 10-hour days. Offices provided a big selection of drinks and snacks. When I was one of the 100 employees based in the Sydney office, hot lunches were catered daily until it was time for Bloomberg to be more careful with its money. Even then, being hungry or thirsty could never be an excuse to leave the office.

Accuracy is crucial. No matter how fast you have to work mistakes are not tolerated. Bloomberg News reporters must follow many rules—including on style, attribution and the construction of stories—that are described in *The Bloomberg Way: A Guide for Reporters and Editors* by Matthew Winkler. There are the five F's ("that define our news organisation: providing the first, fastest, factual, final and future words"), the four-paragraph lead and a list of banned words.

While many journalists scoff at the regimentation of Bloomberg News reporters, I believe it has taught me how to be disciplined with my writing. I've learnt the importance of accuracy, preparation and doing that extra bit of work to make stories stand out.

Above all, it has taught me that using simple and concise language can make for great writing. The lessons I learnt while writing daily stories about financial markets, company news, the economy and monetary policy I still apply in authoring books about endurance sports and writing today. Bloomberg News taught me to dig deeper until you find a satisfying answer, instead of the lazy way out. Stock prices don't fall because investors take profits, a standard term used in business reporting: they fall because investors sell. So why are they selling *today*? They could have waited another day before taking their profits.

Watch for the clichés and explore beyond them by asking what it really means. The potter I interviewed a week ago told me she loves working with clay "because it is therapeutic". That answer didn't tell me anything. The dictionary describes therapeutic as relating to the treating or curing of disease; curative. I didn't use that comment in the story I wrote about her because if it failed to show me, it would fail to show the reader. I had so many other comments from her that were unique and specific.

Exercise: Describe one lesson you have learnt about writing. Also describe when, how and why you learnt it. Next, detail one aspect of your writing you feel you should improve.

TWENTY-FIVE

ADJUSTING

Bah. This morning my writing feels strained. My mind is distracted. Tim and I keep talking about adopting puppy Fred from the local SPCA. In the past two months I have checked the BC SPCA website at least a couple of times a week to see the dogs that are up for adoption. Before seeing Fred I had found one named Tonka, listed as being at the SPCA of the Sunshine Coast. We liked her photo and description.

From Squamish, it takes 45 minutes to drive to the Horseshoe Bay terminal from where you take a ferry to get to the Sunshine Coast. We didn't make the effort before Tonka's listing disappeared from the website which I guess meant someone adopted her. Good for Tonka.

I am thinking more about our potential puppy than about writing. I must try to refocus.

My neck is sore from the two hours I spent power-washing our deck yesterday, a sunny 18-degree-Celsius day in early April. After many litres of water only half the deck looks clean. You can imagine the wood was alive once, now that it is rid of the pale grey colour, I imagine, similar to that of a corpse. I'll aim to do the other half this afternoon.

A fence, which could also do with some high-pressure water treatment, is adding to the sad appearance of our backyard. It's a dodgy pale-red breeding ground for soft-green mosses.

First I'll go for a run. I skipped my training yesterday because the power-washing had left me too tired to deal with a 50-minute run. Today my training program prescribes an 80-minute easy session. Tomorrow I will do the session I was meant to do yesterday, instead of the rest day as my program indicates it to be. Usually I stick to my training program and avoid swapping sessions around.

At least I did type more than 1100 words today already before 9:30 am.

I feel it is a jumbled mess.

At least I wrote. It's time to run.

Exercise: Describe how you are better able now to keep writing, postponing judgement, than you were when you started this book. Be specific and detail your changed approach to writing quantity and how that is helping you. If you feel you haven't changed, then describe so too.

TWENTY-SIX

DISCOVERING

After I started DAY SIX yesterday with highlighting the fact that I was still ahead of my 2000-words-a-day target, I faltered. I allowed myself to be distracted, mostly with our potential adoption of puppy Fred. Emailing my parents, my sister and friends and discussing the pros and cons of having a dog with Tim, my mind was scattered and my writing shows it.

Jumping from topic to topic, I failed to say wanted to say with each one. After I had written 1160 words, I felt annoyed at my lack of focus and decided to clear my mind with a run. Then I had lunch and a good chat with Tim in which we finally settled the question about our puppy.

In the afternoon, I finished the article about the potter, the first I've written in my new role as director of PR & marketing for the group of visual artists in Squamish. She has been a potter for more than 40 years after she obtained a Bachelor of Arts in ceramics. She lives and breathes clay. In the interview, she taught me about pottery and verbalised an approach that can benefit any artist including us as writers.

Her philosophy is that anyone can do well if they put effort into the goals they pursue, in her case throwing clay and even building a 20-cubic-foot gas kiln (which has officially been approved by regulators) in the backyard.

Her potter's eyes are open to learning and to being inspired, whether they are on holiday in Egypt or Mexico or walking along the river in her hometown of Squamish. She is an expert in clay and pottery techniques, yet the first to admit she could never know everything there is to know: the expert is always a willing student. She's continually exploring ways to advance her art and to sustain her path of discovery and improvement.

Working on her story helped remind me that the journey is what matters. Each step you take towards your goal is a step worth taking, even if it doesn't turn out the way you want or expect. It's about exploring that vision, taking chances and enjoying the discoveries you make along the way. They will help inform your passion, and fuel it.

Exercise: Describe what you have explored and discovered while completing the exercises in this book. Detail how they have informed and fuelled your passion for writing.

TWENTY-SEVEN

SURPRISING

My running consists of training and races. In the last four years I've competed in six to 10 races every year. While each race is important, I focus on one key event every six months and compete in the others as preparation. Since 2006 my goal races have been marathons. Distance running requires consistent training of body and mind, especially if you seek to improve. Since most runners love to run they generally also love to train. That said, the sessions that challenge one's body to run fast or far can be demanding and how you approach these mentally will greatly affect your performance. When you race a marathon your frame of mind will largely determine the outcome, provided you have prepared your body as well as possible.

Striking the right balance between being relaxed and focused is crucial on race day: your mind needs to be free from strain to be able to concentrate on the task at hand. You have to be able to psyche yourself into running hard for those 42.195km to achieve your goal, yet avoid focusing on the outcome because you need to concentrate on the process to maximise your performance.

The key to marathon racing is the ability to apply your energy to the present, to focus on every step especially during the later stages in the race when your body is approaching exhaustion and your mind will convince you to stop if you let it. That's when you experience the hardest and most enjoyable aspect of distance running: emptying your mind from any past and future to focus on making the present the best it can be.

As writers we also need to learn to relax so we write without giving in to the critic in our head and sustain our effort long enough to finish that first draft. We must concentrate on what is important now, writing word after word, sentence after sentence so we can fill page after page.

The other day I came across an online reference to a book titled *Wabi Sabi for Writers* by Richard Powell. Intrigued by the words Wabi Sabi, I found it was a Japanese concept described on the author's website as, "An intuitive way of living that involves noticing the moments that make life rich and paying attention to the simple pleasures that can be overshadowed by the bustle and excess of our consumer society." The reminder to observe such moments and pleasures is a useful one, including for our writing.

I run, most of all, because it is what I love to do. Being a runner (and previously a triathlete) has also increased my understanding of who I am and who I can be. Preparing for and racing marathons is fun, exciting and an exercise in self-control, focus and determination. I approach them with a mixture of confidence, excitement and fear. I love the promise of possibility at the start line and the sense of accomplishment at the finish for having tried and conquered. Anything is possible—if you try.

117

One day I may complete a marathon in less than 3 hours. One day I may be the first female across a marathon finish line. I may not accomplish these things but I certainly won't if I decide beforehand that they are not going to happen and therefore I am not going to even try. [Within two months of writing the first draft for this book I won the 2009 North Olympic Discovery Marathon in the US and set a female course record.]

By the same token, write if you enjoy expressing ideas and telling stories in language on paper. In the process, you may finish a book, or publish one or become a best-selling author. You won't know until you try.

I have spent the last 3 ½ months training specifically for the Vancouver Marathon, which I am to run in three weeks: everything I have done since I first tried running in Brussels in 1996 and stuck with it has been a preparation for this race.

I know what to expect on race day because of my experience in previous marathons, including one on the same course. But I also know that this day will be unique—no other marathon before and after will be the same. I will apply the lessons I have learnt from being a runner for more than 13 years. My behaviour and thoughts during my 10th marathon will reflect the cumulative experience of the previous nine. I can visualise the start. Last year the Vancouver Marathon began on a sunny, chilly

Sunday morning. It was easy to get a spot near the front of the start line. I will do the same this year.

I already know what I will be wearing. Clothing must be comfortable. Nothing should chafe, rub or impair your movements in any way. You need to wear something so comfortable that it allows you not to think about it. Race nutrition is very important and it affects my choice of outfit because I need to carry eight energy gels, of which I will have one every 15 minutes after the first hour of running, in my clothing without discomfort.

On a training run three weeks ago, the packaging of the energy gels I brought had rough and pointy edges. I always carry those gels in the back pockets of a tight-fitting top. As I started running one of the gels scratched lightly against my skin. I didn't think much of it but by the time my three-hour run was done it had caused a small raw and bleeding wound. Minor discomforts can turn into major pains over a long-distance run.

As a general rule, your equipment—shoes, socks, shorts, top and hat—will not make you run any faster than you have trained your body to do but it can definitely slow you down if it causes discomfort. Such preventable problems distract, thwarting you from performing to your true potential. A few of my own experiences include a hat so shallow the slightest breeze risked blowing it away (Canberra marathon 2007), shoes barely used in training causing knee pain that reduced me to a walk (Frankfurt Ironman 2005), chafing of a top that left scars for weeks (too many training days and races to recall), eating unusual food the day before a race causing stomach upsets and multiple stops along the course (Forster Ironman 2003).

You learn from these experiences and see the truth in the athlete's adage, Don't try anything—and I mean anything—new on race day.

Exercise: Write down the first adage that comes to mind. Think quick, spontaneity is good. Now describe how this familiar truth applies to your writing. As always, be specific and detailed and keep writing until you meet at least your daily word goal.

TWENTY-EIGHT

AFFIRMING

If someone asked me to run a marathon right this minute, I could. I'd know exactly which clothes to grab, which shoes to wear, where to rub a good layer of Vaseline on my feet before donning my favourite running socks, which and how many energy gels and energy bars to take, how to warm up, what pace to race the marathon at and how to find that speed. In the past four years, as a runner I've been a marathoner first and foremost. That race distance gets me excited and motivated to head out the door every day to complete my training.

In writing we also need to find the goal that inspires us to hone our skills every day. It doesn't mean that we are always excited about committing words to the page or that it is going to be easy. And that's OK. As long as we can keep tapping into that passion and remind ourselves that we are getting better with each effort, we can sustain ourselves through the challenges.

Today my session is a 50-minute easy run. That means I should run at a pace that feels comfortable, so my breathing should be relaxed and I should not feel strained in any way. Over the next three weeks my training volume drops, or in other words my so-called taper starts. A marathon runner tapers so she can be as rested and fresh as possible on race day, both mentally and physically.

While the overall distance I train declines in the final three weeks before the marathon, I will keep doing two speed sessions per week, including a 3km time trial next Tuesday which I have to run as fast as I can. My coach wants me to complete it in 11 minutes and 20 seconds, or faster. That means I have to cover each kilometre in 3 minutes and 45 seconds, or faster. (By comparison, in my fastest marathon I needed 4 minutes and 26 seconds for each kilometre.)

In the 3km time trial I will be comfortable during the first 500 metres—this is where I aim to find my pace. In the second 500 metres, I will feel a little discomfort—if not, I can speed up slightly. After a kilometre I will check whether I am on pace—at this stage being 5 seconds slower is better than 5 seconds faster.

The worst-case scenario is if I am running more than 5 seconds slower than my target pace, yet feel it's a higher effort than I can sustain. The best-case scenario is that I am ahead of my target pace, experiencing no discomfort and feeling as if I can stick to that pace for another 2km. The most likely scenario is that I am on target and feel a level of discomfort that is manageable.

The physical part of these sessions is naturally very important. You need to tune into your body. Relaxing is crucial. As the effort feels increasingly uncomfortable over the duration of the time trial my focus will be on my breathing as that is essential to staying calm and in control when we feel under pressure. My self-talk must remain positive and enabling, especially in that final 500 metres of the time trial as I aim to make the most of my current level of fitness. Our mind determines whether we will succeed, be it running or writing. Perception is everything.

Remember the last time you woke up from a nightmare, sweating with your heart pounding. Your body responded as if it were in real danger, in an event that only happened in your dream, your mind. Once awake and realising you're safely in your own bed, you relax as your mind sends the message that it was only a nightmare. The mind controls the body.

As writers we must remember this too. We must think about our writing in a way that is positive and enabling to get the most out of ourselves as we fill the page. Do not let negativity take charge of your mind. Practice positive self-talk every day when you write.

Yesterday a friend told me in an email that she loved my second book. "And I was pleased to see your picture on the back cover too—now you aren't anonymous anymore and people can start stopping you in the street to congratulate you on your inspirational books," she wrote.

Her comment made me laugh. I feel a long way off from being stopped in the street by people who love the books I write. On second thought, I decided to make it part of my visualisation as a writer. If we believe we can achieve.

Nearly always does our capability surpass our expectations if we try honestly. During my running time trial, mental checklists help me stay calm and perform my best: I make sure my face feels relaxed, my teeth aren't clenched, my shoulders feel loose, my back is relaxed and that my legs are turning over quickly at the most efficient pace.

In challenges of any kind, including writing a book, controlling your state of mind is crucial. You must stay positive—especially when that is difficult. In the last kilometre of my time trial I will be tempted to slow down as my level of discomfort increases. This is the final stretch which—no matter what distance you run—is always going to be the hardest if you are aiming to do as well as you can.

I use affirmations like, Relax and achieve the max, to help me focus and stick to my pace. I must control thoughts about how hard or how uncomfortable it is and replace them with a positive sentence that reminds me to stay in the moment like, Quick feet.

Some people have a higher tolerance of discomfort than others. I'd be curious to know how someone else's capacity to endure pain during athletic efforts compares to mine: is it as varied as I expect it to be or is it actually pretty similar? For example, does someone like marathon world record holder Paula Radcliffe feel the same level of discomfort as an average marathoner striving for a personal best time?

I find it mentally, and physically, easier to do a three-hour run at a moderate pace than a 3km time trial in 11 minutes. In other words, I'd rather hurt less for longer than hurt more for a shorter period of time. My body may cope better with longer distances or perhaps it is again the power of the mind: because I *think* I deal better with running longer distances, I do. A self-fulfilling prophesy.

Exercise: Describe your thoughts when you feel you are writing well. Detail how such positive self-talk helps you sustain you in your writing. Keep going by listing what your strengths are as a writer. Be specific and exhaustive. At the end of this exercise create three positive sentences, or affirmations, that apply to your strengths as a writer. Display these in a place near your desk so you will be reminded of these daily.

TWENTY-NINE

SUSTAINING

People will often comment that a 10-kilometre race must be easy for a marathoner. The distance can be—if that marathoner chooses to run it at a comfortable pace. However, in races you usually try to cover the distance, whether it is 10km or 42.195km, as swift as possible. One of my favourite quotes is by Alberto Salazar who won the 1982 Boston Marathon after a legendary neck-and-neck battle with Dick Beardsley and set a course record in the process: "You will run your best races at a pace that you can barely sustain."

If I run a 10km race at the same pace that I use to do a marathon, the shorter event would be easier indeed. You can run at a quicker pace for a shorter distance. In my 10km races I will take 4 minutes to cover each kilometre. In my marathons I take 4 minutes and 26 seconds, or longer. Twenty-six seconds per kilometre may not sound like much of a difference but, trust me, it is.

The true art of racing is finding your optimal pace for that specific distance and course on that particular day. You cannot start by going all out because you would only last, say, 100 metres. If you start too slow you will complete the course with energy left in the tank. You must take accumulating fatigue into account and find the highest speed you can maintain until the finish line: ideally you avoid running out of steam before then.

That optimal pace varies per runner, race, day, distance, course, weather, preparation, and so on. Each result is influenced by many factors so you'd better control the ones you can. And don't worry about the ones you cannot.

Improving upon previous achievements is a work in progress. Always remember, errors are part of trials. Making mistakes can benefit us if we learn from them so we can do better the next time.

Exercise: Describe the sustainable pace you have found as a writer. Take into account the number of days per week that you are consistently writing, the number of words you write per session and the time you have allocated for writing in your schedule. Write about how and why that has changed in recent weeks. Describe mistakes and what you have learnt in the process of exploring your writing pace. If you feel you haven't found that optimal pace yet, detail what you are struggling with and how you can improve.

THIRTY

RECOLLECTING

It's 7:30am on Easter Friday. The sun is slowly rising from behind the mountains I see from the bedroom window. I am writing at the small desk by the large master bedroom window facing south and overlooking the backyard, which consists of a flat rectangle separated from a steep ravine with mature trees by a fence. While the ravine is unusable, it's ours and guarantees our privacy on the southern side. It is one of the main reasons we chose this house.

Spring has sprung after a winter with plenty of snow, which is a-typical for Squamish. Squirrels and chipmunks are the first ones to appear, gathering food. Birds are singing about the happiest part of the year holding the promise of new life and a warm summer.

Tim and I are also excited about a new start. After months of contemplation, we have decided to bring a dog into our life. Inspired by a couple we know in Australia who have three dogs of which they rescued two from the pound, we wanted to give a stray dog a home too. We didn't have to think long about all the reasons to adopt a canine.

Tim and I both grew up with dogs in our respective families. When I was born my parents had a Scottish Collie named Max, a beautiful dog who believed guarding the family was important. A few months after Max died of old age, a Kuvasz puppy arrived in our home. This Hungarian breed

131

has its independent spirit. My parents named him Tabor. I was less than 10 years old and fell in love with him immediately

I remember him peeing on my leg. Wearing an orange dress on a sunny day, I realised he was using my leg as a tree when I felt a warm liquid running down my skin. Everyone else laughed, so I did too. He was just a puppy after all.

Tabor was a high-energy dog. He and I loved playing for hours in our yard that was only separated by a transparent fence from the harbour of Harderwijk, which was part of the Hanseatic League of trading cites from the 13th through the 17th centuries. Summers were great as we spent a lot of time outside in that yard next to the water.

Our next dog was an Irish Wolfhound named Ascot, named after the race course for reasons I still do not understand. This dog was as sweet as he was huge. What I remember most about him are the comments he drew from strangers. Our family including Ascot stayed in a holiday park called Slagharen, which is themed around ponies and horses. Staying in one of the park's cabins, we heard the joke that ours came with a pony more than once. Walking a dog with a shoulder height of 90 centimetres (and weighing 70 kilograms) didn't appear out of proportion for my dad who is 187cm. It was a different story for my mum, who is 165cm.

Since I moved away from home, my parents have had two Bearded Collies including their current dog Thara. She has such a happy and gentle disposition. Her all-over fawn coat is rare and gorgeous. My mum spends at least an hour once a week brushing Thara's long hair—patience required from both parties.

Thara also knows to put her front paws on a square ottoman every morning so my mum can comb the long hair on top of her head away from her eyes and tie it into a pony tail or braid. While the hairdo is done so she can see better, it looks very cute too.

Thara's nature is different from that of Iris, my parents' previous Bearded Collie who came from the same breeder, named Imke. Imke, who I have met once at a dog show in the Netherlands, fell in love with Bearded Collies in her early teens and started breeding them. She now has nine Bearded Collies which she shows across Europe and has raised several champion dogs. And she is only 24. My parents attend the annual walks Imke organises for the people who have bought a puppy from one of her litters. An avid photographer, Imke maintains a great website for her Braemoor kennel.

My parents got Thara as a puppy a couple of years after Iris, who was a quiet dog, died of cancer at the age of 10. While my parents, who were then in their mid-60s, knew from experience that puppies are hard work, Thara's high energy caught them by surprise. They have risen to the challenge. Thara is walked four times a day, every day, usually by my dad though she is considered to be my mum's dog.

Exercise: Choose a clear memory from childhood and describe how it is relevant to your life today. You can take any road you like. Be specific and keep writing.

THIRTY-ONE

ELABORATING

My sister Angelique got her Jack Russell named Punky just after I'd moved to Canada for the first time in 1998 so I missed sharing that experience with her. Angelique watched Punky being born to one of the three Jack Russells of good friends of hers, who then gave him to her as a surprise birthday gift when he was eight weeks old. She and Punky have been inseparable since.

Angelique has always loved animals. When we were little, she and I went to a birthday party of her best friend. The afternoon included a visit to the cinema to watch *Bambi*. Angelique and I were five and eight years old respectively. During the scene where fire destroys the forest where Bambi and his friends live, all animals flee for their lives. Not all survive which was more than my sister could handle. She was so upset her friend's mum took her out of the theatre before the movie ended.

We had a few cats growing up. The first one was a beautiful kitten which we got from our neighbours under the condition our Scottish Collie Max would get along with it. My sister and I loved it. Unfortunately Max did not.

A couple of years later my mum noticed a litter with stray kittens behind the locked gates of one of the factories on our street when she was walking Ascot. It was a Sunday. She walked home to get my sister and I, and a basket. The three of us walked back to the factory where my mum had seen the litter. My mum climbed over the fence and found that there were three kittens. She handed them to us through the fence before climbing back over it. We took them home, and to the vet the next day who said they were sick. One was blind and too ill to recover so our vet advised to put her down. The other two, both black and white, went home with us where my sister named hers Tommy and I named mine Mineke.

During the day Tommy and Mineke were free to go outside. At night the cats stayed inside where Mineke's preference was to sleep in my bed, snuggled up against my tummy. One night Mineke didn't come home. No amount of calling and searching helped. I never saw her again nor found out what happened. I was devastated.

Shortly before I left home to obtain a Bachelor of Commerce degree, which in the Netherlands takes four years, Tommy got company from a new kitten who we named Kyra. Tommy lived to be an old cat with scars marking his face from the fights he always seemed to get into with his stray friends. If my dad stayed late at the office, which was next to our house, Tommy would go over and sit outside until my dad closed up. They then walked home together.

Kyra, who always found my lap when I was home for the weekend or the holiday, saw the age of 18. She died only a couple of years ago.

Exercise: Elaborate on one of the topics linked to the childhood memory you used for the exercise of the previous chapter.

THIRTY-TWO

VISUALISING

I remember our neighbour trying to console me after I was told our Kuvasz Tabor had been put down at 10 months because he had attacked my dad in our house, leaving him with 22 bites in his arm, a number I've never forgotten. (Three other dogs from the same litter as Tabor were also put down for aggressive behaviour.) The dog that I was so fond of had been taken away after such a short period of time, just like my cat Mineke.

My sister's Jack Russell is 11 now and my parents' Bearded Collie is four. Both dogs are high energy, smart and a lot of fun. Tim's parents have had a Schnauzer for years and they adore their dog too. One of Tim's sisters has a couple of miniature Schnauzers which currently both are pregnant.

Until recently, the lifestyle of Tim and I chose was not conducive to having any pets. We worked long hours and moved every few years. In the last 20 years I've lived in eight different cities in four countries at more than 20 different addresses.

Tim and I have travelled a lot, before and since we met. Of the past five years, we spent nearly two of them travelling. Our close relatives live in the Netherlands, Canada, the US and Turkey, while good friends reside in Australia, the UK, the United Arab Emirates and Singapore.

In the last 18 months much has changed. While we still work long hours, we now do so from the home we bought recently. In some ways we are still finding our feet in this new lifestyle. We've moved to a new town where we didn't know anyone. We have met nice people here and are starting to make new friends.

Tim and I each cherish our independence and lead busy lives, always working towards the next goal. Given our nomadic lifestyle so far it feels strange to have bought a home in Squamish as moving from here would involve a lot more than simply giving notice to a landlord and packing up.

We didn't know much more about the town than that it is small (pop. 16,000); surrounded by mountains and next to Howe Sound, North America's southernmost fjord; and lies between Vancouver and Whistler. We're unlikely to travel as extensively as we have in the past five years: we will spend our holidays in North America and could easily take the car, and therefore a dog, in the next few years. Tim and I visit our respective families regularly but tend do so separately to ease the strain on our budget. So one of us will be home to take care of a dog and would then have company too instead of being home alone.

Hearing the rain tonight I say to Tim, Your turn to walk the dog. We laugh, before mentioning doggy nails scratching our kitchen's new $2500 bamboo floor, one of the biggest renovation splurges in our house. Oh well. Our decision is made: we'll head to the SPCA in Squamish tomorrow to adopt puppy Fred.

Exercise: Describe the store, or any place, where you would most like to see your book on the shelves. Detail your book's exact place on a shelf as well as where the building is located, what kind of building it is, and your reasons for wanting a copy of your book there, of all places. Be as specific as you can be, such as whether it is for sale and the book's physical journey to get there.

THIRTY-THREE

CELEBRATING

The original plan for my 10-day challenge was to write a 20,000-word manuscript. I wrote on DAY EIGHT but didn't on DAY NINE nor on DAY TEN. Just like any employee is expected to show up at work, barring illness or any other emergencies, writers need to put words to the page without excuses aimed at justifying not having done so.

I didn't fall ill on DAY NINE, nor did I have any emergencies that would have provided a valid excuse for failing to meet the goals of the 10-day writing challenge. I allowed my priorities to shift, as we adopted four-month-old puppy Fred, which we named Luka, and brought him home that day. (That's a whole new book.)

Exercise: It is time to take stock. If you have done your writing exercises on a computer, use the word count function to verify if you have met your quantity goal set at the start of this book. If you have written longhand count the number of pages you have filled in your journal or notepad, and compare this with your original target. Describe the sense of accomplishment you feel. Detail the lessons you feel you have learnt over the past 32 sessions and how you will apply them to your writing in the future. Celebrate your achievement.

Recommended reads

The Sound of Paper: Starting from Scratch
by Julia Cameron

The Courage to Write: How Writers Transcend Fear
by Ralph Keyes

On Writing Well: the Classic Guide to Writing Nonfiction
by William Zinsser

Bird by Bird: Some Instructions on Writing and Life
by Anne Lamott

In Pursuit of Excellence: How to Win in Sport and Life Through Mental Training
by Terry Orlick

A Moveable Feast
by Ernest Hemingway

Writing Down the Bones: Freeing the Writer Within
by Natalie Goldberg

Between Trapezes: Flying into a New Life With the Greatest of Ease
by Gail Blanke

About the author

Margreet Dietz was born in the Netherlands in 1970. After completing a Bachelor of Commerce degree, she began a career in marketing only to realise she wanted to be a writer. She quit her job in 1995 and went back to university, moving to Brussels, Belgium, where she obtained a Master in International and Comparative Law. In 1996 she started working as a reporter at Bloomberg News in its Brussels office, followed by stints in Toronto, Canada, and subsequently Sydney, Australia. She left Bloomberg News in 2004 to travel and compete in endurance sports events around the world including three Ironman triathlons. She received a Distinction for the Book Editing and Publishing course she took in 2005. In 2006 she became a copy-editor at *The Australian Financial Review* in Sydney, and began writing for endurance sports magazines. She and long-time partner Tim moved to the West Coast of Canada at the end of 2007, where she started researching and writing her first book, *Running Shoes Are a Girl's Best Friend*, published in November 2009. Her second book *Powered From Within: Stories About Running & Triathlon* is a collection of 13 of her magazine articles. Margreet now lives with Tim and their dog Luka in Squamish, BC, where she is working on her next book. This is her third.

Made in the USA
Charleston, SC
07 May 2010